Celebrate the Mommy Milestones™

Lanelle Vasichek

Illustrations by Annette Wood
Edited by Carol McAdoo Rehme

Requests for permission should be addressed to:
Olive Publishing Group, LLC
PO BOX 1602
Fargo, ND 58107-1602

Illustrations and Design by Annette Wood.
annettewoodgraphics.com

Ordering Information:
Special discounts are available on quantity purchases by corporations, associations, and others. For details, contact the publisher at the address above.

Orders by U.S. trade bookstores and wholesalers, please contact
Olive Publishing Group, LLC:
Phone: 701-219-1699 or visit www.mommymilestones.com

Printed in the United States.

First edition

ISBN#: 978-0-9862797-0-6

To my bosses,
Michael and Katelyn

Contents

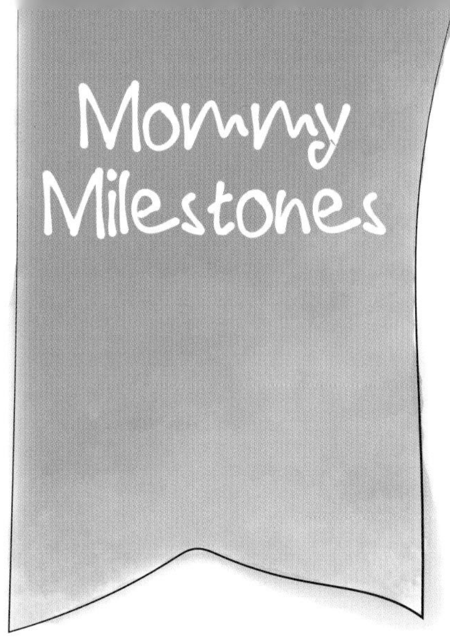

Mommy Milestones are the breakthroughs moms achieve but don't take time to notice, let alone celebrate. Some milestones are life-changing; a few we would like to forget; even so, we ~~survive~~ reach them, take a deep breath and move on.

It's important to know we're not alone in the ~~crazy~~ precious world of motherhood. It's equally important to recognize that within the everyday moments, we moms are accomplishing big things. Our decisions, our actions, our responsibilities grow —and our world changes. These accomplishments are something to be proud of and feel awesome about.

Whether you've have had a baby, have friends who have babies, or are one of the very special men who ~~stay out of the way~~ stand strong in support, it's time to sit back and recognize all the moments to celebrate within the painfully brave and oh-so-true journey of the Mommy Milestones.

Enjoy!

mile (mī(-ə)l) *n.* 1. a unit of distance on land in English-speaking countries equal to 5280 feet, or 1760 yards. 2. a stretch goal for any new mommy to run.

mile·stone (mīlˌstōn) *n.* plural: milestones 1. an action or event marking a significant change or stage in development.

mil·i·ar·ia (mi-lē-ˈer-ē-ə) *n.* 1. an inflammatory disorder of the skin that is characterized by redness, and burning or itching due to blockage of sweat gland ducts.2. a condition you should steer clear of, if at all possible.

I had everything figured out. I had a plan for my life, and—lucky me—everything seemed to fall right into place:

MY MASTER PLAN
Do Well in School
Find the perfect haircut
Meet a smart, good looking boy
Get married
Live happily ever after

We lived a honeymoon existence for quite some time and enjoyed every selfish moment of it. Who wouldn't? Is there anyone who doesn't love traveling, eating out, and engaging in spontaneous excursions with plenty of free time to spare? Everything was exactly as I had envisioned. Charmed.

And the cherry on top? I was fortunate to have an amazing group of friends collected through all the crazy stages of my life. As we became self-proclaimed grown-ups, new little people were introduced into our circle. It was an exciting era as they started their families.

ANNOUNCING: The Newest Person in the World!

Surprisingly, visits with our friends who had made the big leap into parenthood left my husband and I a little ~~nauseated~~ stunned. If our conversations lasted longer than forty-three seconds, the topic (regardless of how it started) inevitably circled back to their babies. It seemed this was the only subject worth talking about—complete with endless details about feedings, schedules, and bodily fluids from both baby and mom.

Me: How are you?

Friend: Our new baby is amazing!

How are you feeling?

You have no idea how life changing blah-blah baby blah-blah poopie diapers, blah-blah.

Uh huh.

Smelly blah-blah smiling blah-blah bleeding blah-blah poop again blah-blah exhausted and awesome blah-blah-blah.

That's nice. Wow, look at the time!

I was convinced my friends had been steered wrong, abandoning their former carefree lives for a world in which I didn't even recognize them. Their houses were hazardous jungles waiting to nab the next unsuspecting visitor, an unwilling participant in its obstacle course, which smelled suspiciously like sour milk. What was it we'd once had in common?

My husband and I left these visits in silence, but as soon as the car doors closed (in the hope of sound-proofing our every thought and word) our tongues raced.

Who were those people?
Can't they discuss anything other than their kids?
Have they forgotten about all their interests?
Don't they realize how sticky everything is?

By the time we arrived home, my heart rate calmed and I sank into deep thought about my own beloved life.

I know my world isn't perfect.
Granted, at times I could be a livelier conversationalist.
My attention span for topics unrelated
to my life could be longer.

Sure, I can really make messes, but if anything is sticky, it's supposed to be that way.

I was convinced: When the time came for *us* to take the leap into parenthood—to invite a little person into our pleasantly orchestrated environment—he would enjoy good food and good music and have an appreciation for a good night's sleep.

"When *we* have kids it's going to be different," we vowed.

I had heard it a thousand times: *Having a baby is a life-changing event.* I wondered how many people were seriously *hoping* for a life-changing event to come their way. I could think of a few things I would welcome with open arms.

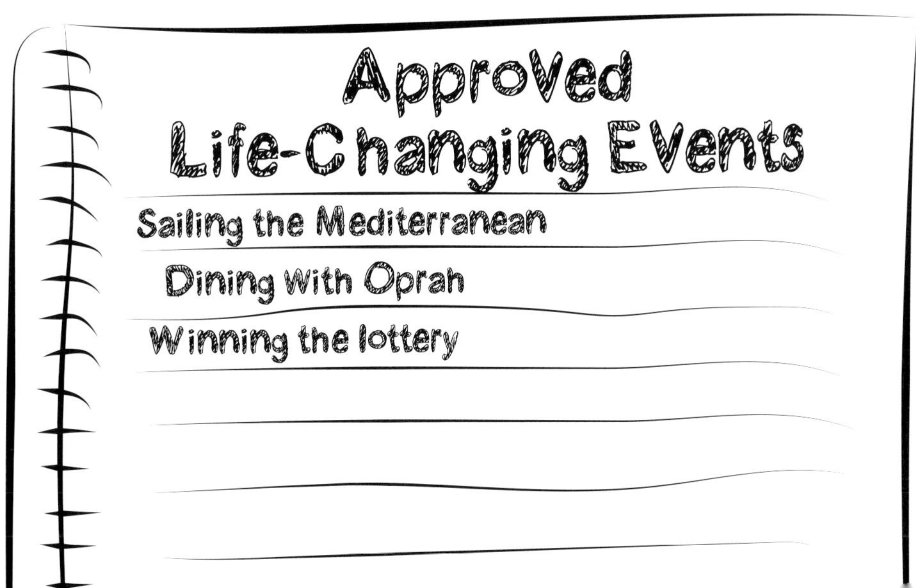

Approved
Life-Changing Events
Sailing the Mediterranean
Dining With Oprah
Winning the lottery

I was betting there weren't many guarantees in the world of life-changing. A sure bet? It was going to be serious, with no going back to the way things were. So we waited years to have kids, years filled with trips around the world, indulging our whims and interests, and conversing—long and intimately—over pints in our favorite pubs. We rolled out our own vision of the future.

Him: I love our life.

Me: I agree. Our life is awesome.

Let's not get all crazy and change our world just because we have a baby.

Agreed. Keep everything the same. Just add a little person to the party!

So glad we are on the same page.

<enter baby>

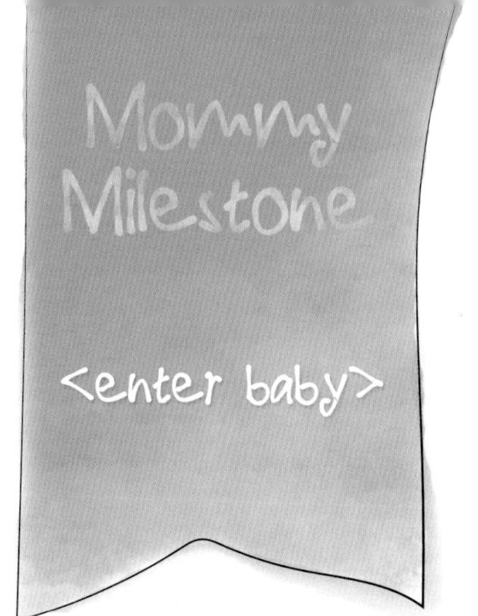

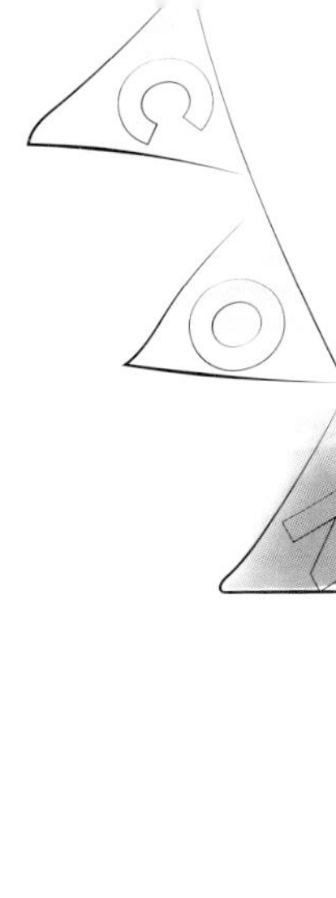

Every mom has a story about The Big Day. And, it's virtually impossible for a woman to listen to someone's birthing story without adding her own tale. I admit to testing this theory every now and again by asking one gal in the group about her big event and watching how quickly the rest of the moms ~~competed~~ jumped in. I've thought about sending in a skit suggestion for the team at Saturday Night Live for their next "One-Upper" episode, although it might be difficult for even the professionals to exaggerate what happens in real-life.

Birthing stories vary from:

- natural to Cesarean
- difficult to impossible
- crazy-quick to forever-and-a-day (or more)
- painful to more staggering than you can possibly imagine

One thing we all agree on: There really isn't an easy way to get a ~~watermelon~~ baby out of your body.

I have my own story, and I promise not to bore you with the details of dilation and pushes. What I will elaborate on was the astonishing number of people who visited the hospital—while I was ~~gasping~~ fresh from my final push.

I will take ownership of a tiny bit of the ridiculousness. I will admit to giving the first time daddy the go-ahead to spread the good news to grandparents. And I admit notifying my office not to expect me for roughly twelve weeks. But that is where the telephone game stopped. Any other announcements didn't come from *our* direction. I soon realized I'd lost any last-grasp control of my charmed world.

I found those short days in the hospital ~~uncomfortable~~ ~~overwhelming~~ intense. The nurses meant business; I had to learn not to take anything personally. Measuring pain medication, checking vitals on the hour, teaching me how to clamp a baby to my boob, plastering ice packs to my sore bum, asking curious questions around passing gas and my peeing schedule. Well, it was a bit more than any first timer could have been prepared for. Yet, when Grandma and Grandpa arrived to meet the newest member of the family, the awkwardness in the room—hard as it is to believe—escalated.

ATTENTION PEOPLE:

I am in a hospital.

In a very small room.

With nowhere for you to sit.

Minutes after my body survived the most amazing feat to ever challenge it, you want to stop in to chitchat?

How 'bout we just pretend you did?

I sat as motionless as possible in my hospital bed, every scrap of energy concentrated on the certainty of a gush of blood with any movement. Crossing fingers *and* knees, I hoped I wouldn't leak through the enormous pad (stuck to the disposable underwear wrapping my butt) onto the stark white sheets. (gush) Statue-still, I wondered why it wasn't obvious that visitors should leave the room when a nurse, all business, walked in for my maintenance check. I would have skedaddled out of there if I could have gotten away with it.

SERIOUSLY PEOPLE:

You are not being offered an option to stay.
Trust me, it is not going to be pretty.
This is a big fat hint to leave so the nurse can check
my lumpy, black-and-blue, hemorrhoid-invaded butt.
(gush)

Could it get any crazier?

Apparently so.

In popped obscure cousins, who didn't even know I was pregnant, with their own ~~monkeys~~ precious children—who were excited to climb all over ~~me~~ the bed to push ~~my~~ the buttons with their ~~grubby~~ chubby hands and eat what was left of my (now) cold lunch. I tried my best to remain calm. (gush) Impossibly, the madness worsened. My co-workers and office manager arrived. (gush) Hadn't anyone heard about the concept of just sending flowers?

Already exhausted and with nothing left to be bashful about, I powered through until the next day, when I obeyed the nurse's "suggestion" to post a note on my door.

ATTENTION:
This patient may or may not be taking a nap.
We know you are very important, so please leave a message at the nurses' station.

Thank You.

<cue angels singing>

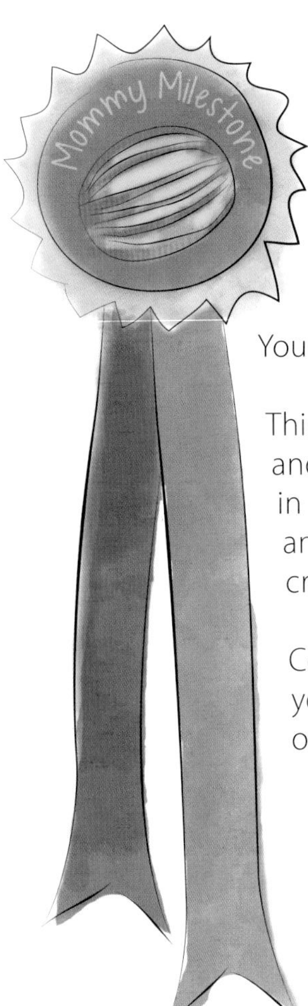

You created a beautiful miracle!

This milestone is filled to the brim with well wishes and best intentions. But it's easy to get caught up in the craziness of gifts and guests, compliments and comments, oohs and ahhs, all while leaking a crimson puddle.

Celebrate by setting aside a quiet time to catch your breath and absorb one of the biggest days of your life.

Mommy Milestone
Milk ... It's What's for Dinner

I realize and appreciate that everyone has been given the gift of free will, but when it comes right down to it, there are a lot of strong opinions about the choices we make for our infants. Whether prenatal appointments, talks with trusted friends, or unsolicited input from complete strangers, breastfeeding conversations went something along the lines of:

So are you planning to be a good mom?

Excuse me?

Or are you going to give your baby (gasp) formula?

Uh....

All cards on the table, I found the formula route had a lot going for it. Not only could everyone have the honor of feeding this new precious person (and who wouldn't want to share that experience with grandma?), mommy could rest easy. She would know exactly how much liquid entered that little body without worrying about her supply meeting his demands. Anyway I looked at it, I was in a no-lose situation.

Caving to peer pressure, I decided nursing was one of the most valuable things I could do. What's to argue? I read the studies' claims; breastfed babies were smarter, stronger, faster, taller, more charismatic, and guaranteed to be voted Most Likely to Succeed on graduation day.

My husband and I registered for a complimentary class sponsored by the hospital: Breastfeeding 101. We sat in a room filled with parents-to-be, anxious to learn about the beautiful and natural art of nursing. After watching the introductory video—which clearly demonstrated various positions and debunked the mystery surrounding latching on—I was certain my ~~tools~~ fixtures were neither prepared nor qualified for the job they were about to embark upon.

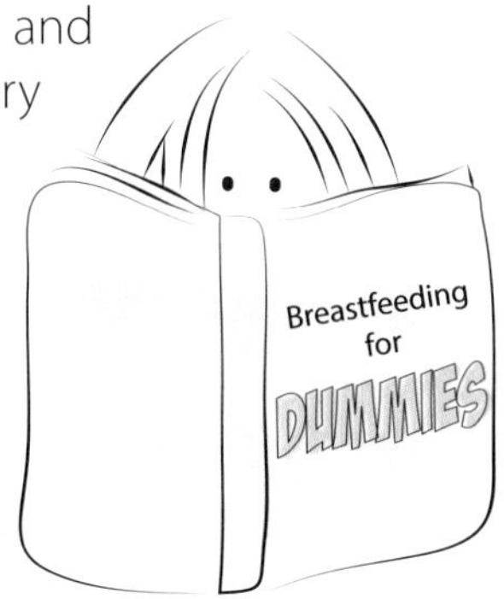

Are my boobs even going to work for this?

For starters, the moms in the video were, ah, extremely blessed. This concerned me because, comparatively, I could be mistaken for a preteen. But that wasn't all. The moms in the video were *multitasking*, for crying out loud.

Really, moms?

I see you have one free hand, but aren't you doing enough? Do you think it's necessary to provide 100% of the nutrition to keep an entire human being alive AND write out your birth announcements? Simultaneously?

Realizing we had just watched the same video, I was pretty certain the expectations of daddies-to-be around the country ~~were warped~~ had been set fairly high. I never thought of myself as an underachiever, but the video made me question my capabilities and strengths and what I was willing to do with my boobs. Although the breastfeeding decision was a milestone I was happy to reach, I had a big-time hunch the process wasn't going to be easy—and that it wouldn't tickle.

Once committed, I embraced my choice, channeled my lactating superpower, and set out to research breast pumps, that vital piece of equipment mandatory for any mom who wanted to nurse her baby and *ever* leave her house. For this privilege, the investment wasn't small. And, unlike the second-hand crib we borrowed from a friend, I wasn't interested in searching Craig's List for a used model.

The dear daddy-to-be made the actual purchase. Top-of-the-line. Only the best for *his* family. A trained engineer, he avidly examined the electronic version of suction—much more exciting to him than yet another conversation about decorating baby's room.

Me: Which color do you think would be best for the nursery?
Him: Did you say something?
Do you have any thoughts on what color we should paint the nursery?
<cue crickets chirping>
Are you ignoring me?
<chirp, chirp>

The moment the pump entered our house, my gem of a man read the entire owner's manual, completely dismantled the apparatus, and proceeded to boil all the parts and pieces. Just like that, it was ready—whether I was or not.

And there goes any chance for returning
this piece of work.

Props to him for giving baby the most nutritional start (some would say) to life. Had it been left to me, that complicated piece of equipment would've gone back to the store long before I'd unpackaged and sanitized it.

Strapping on a breast pump for the first time is a milestone moment burned into my memory.

Am I doing this right?
Will this leave a mark?
And what is the deal with only tiny drops?
The 6-oz. mark on the bottle
is starting to look like a cruel joke.
This has to be one of the most unnatural acts
EVER.

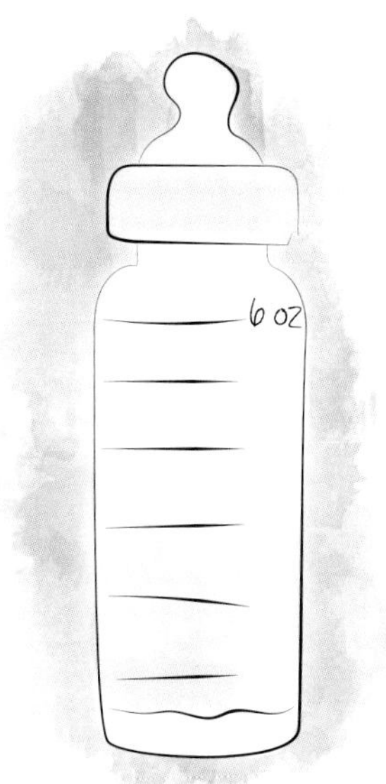

It took a few ~~months~~ feedings for me to get used to the utter vulnerability of having a mechanized contraption strapped to the part of my body previously used for more sensual purposes. Like childbirth, breastfeeding was an instant drain on my shredded modesty. But, at the end of the day, if I ever wanted to leave the babe's side, this modern marvel was a precious gift of freedom. Like the milk it collected, the pump was worth its weight in gold.

One measly drip at a time.

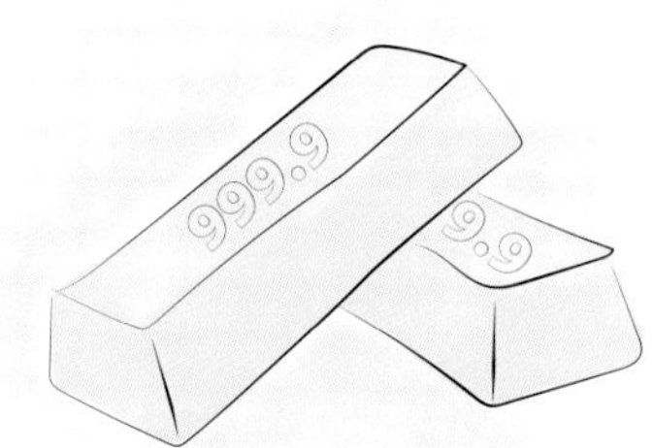

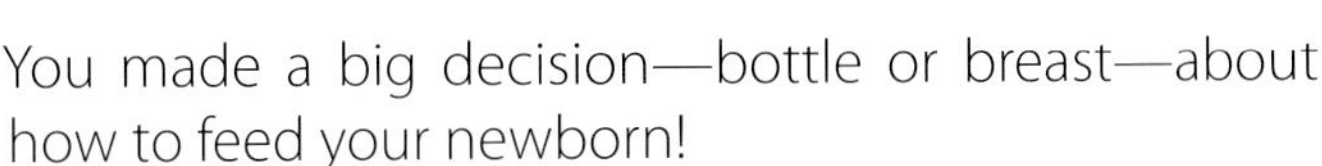

You made a big decision—bottle or breast—about how to feed your newborn!

You did your homework, listened to countless opinions of friends, family, and strangers. Now, be confident in your choice, knowing your decision was right for you and your baby.

Celebrate by taking a selfie with your sophisticated pump or sit back and take a picture of daddy warming the bottle!

Mommy
Milestone
Home Again,
Home Again,
Jiggity-Jig

I am sure I didn't fully appreciate my time in the hospital. The days were a blur of nurses bringing baby for feedings, calls to the cafeteria for food to satisfy my cravings, and angels encouraging me to let them take the newborn so I could get some rest. When the insurance allotment for recovery reached maximum limits, it was time to move on.

*If they'd left my butt alone,
pretty sure I would still be there today.*

I slid into ~~maternity~~ comfortable clothes, packed our belongings, snagged a few extra diapers and a handful of raft-size pads. After one last refresher on bathing baby, we were ready for the trip home, home to start our new life as a family of three.

This is what dreams are made of!

After we said good-bye to our sterilized and safe hospital home, we started our adventure in the big world … once we remembered where we parked the car.

For months, I had invested all my ~~anxiety~~ energy into the prized baby book, researching and filling in details certain to be of interest to this new little person fifty years later:

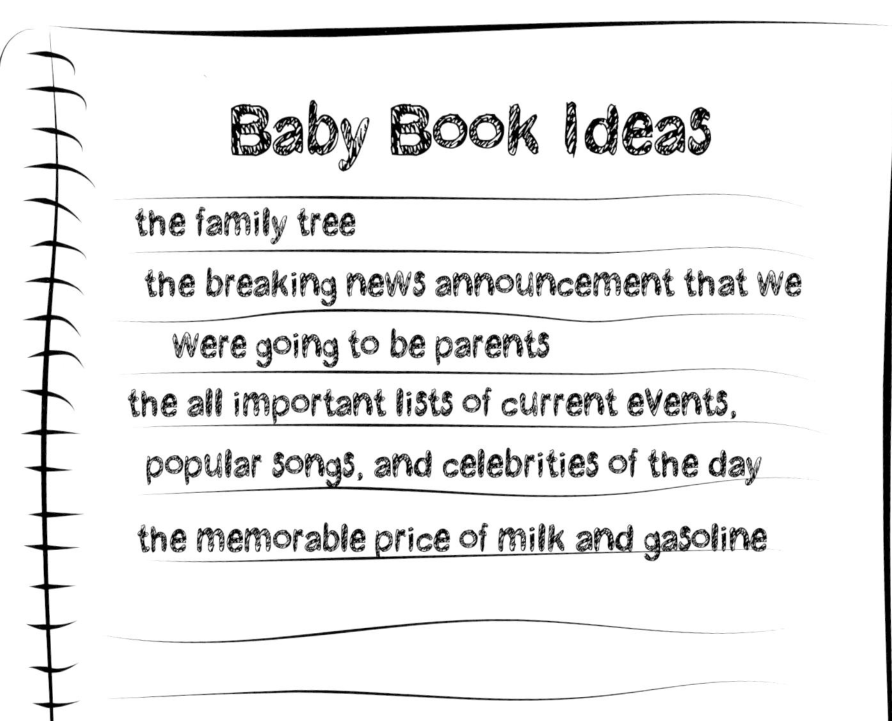

Baby Book Ideas
the family tree
the breaking news announcement that we
were going to be parents
the all important lists of current events,
popular songs, and celebrities of the day
the memorable price of milk and gasoline

Box of Awesomeness

We'd diligently captured each hospital visitor's signature. Even the all-star nurses offered their autographs. The book made Martha Stewart proud.

Delusional, I envisioned a fairytale arrival. Relaxed. Comfortable. Natural. We walked through our familiar front door and … there we stood.

A pile of wrinkled laundry sprawled on the couch, tiredly waiting to be folded. Thirsty plants panted, desperate for water. The dishwasher begged to be loaded. Starving goldfish floated, belly up.

This moment should have been one of the happiest of my life. Balloons, flowers, and congratulatory cards had poured into the house as evidence. I thought about the blank page waiting in the baby book, proof positive: This was a Big Day. I needed to paste on a big smile for the momentous photo.

But before I had unbuckled our new resident from his five-point harness system, reality hit. This was the first day *ever* that I was 100% responsible for someone other than myself. Sure. I sometimes I felt my husband ~~would die without me~~

~~around to feed him~~ would struggle a bit without me. But this was different. This little person's needs now came before mine, and I had a premonition he was going to have a lot. of. needs. I felt a little light-headed. Probably because I had stopped breathing.

Hang with me, mommy.
Start by slipping off your shoes.
No need to panic—just take a deep breath and get a grip.
Babies are born every day to untried parents.
Okay, lie on the floor if you need to. Feet elevated.
Go ahead, loosen the elastic on your pants.

As Daddy unpacked the car, I found myself alone with a tiny stranger. I wasn't scared. I wasn't sad. I was just waiting, waiting to be overcome with joy and love and all the wonderful things an expectant mommy dreams about. Shouldn't the moon and the stars realign to reveal more happiness than I could stand?

Dreams of ...

White fluffy towels magically appearing in my bathroom.
Floors so clean you could see your reflection.
Stuffed animals singing and dancing around the baby.
And where was the stinkin' magical unicorn?

Instead, my house was just as I left it—and worse. I was tired, hungry, and sore. We pulled a soft recliner to the dining room table and began the adventure of learning to eat one-handed. Of discovering that barely-warm food ~~sucks~~ is edible. That fine dining, late night entertaining, sleeping in, and spontaneous outings might need to be carefully planned.

It was time to find our new groove.

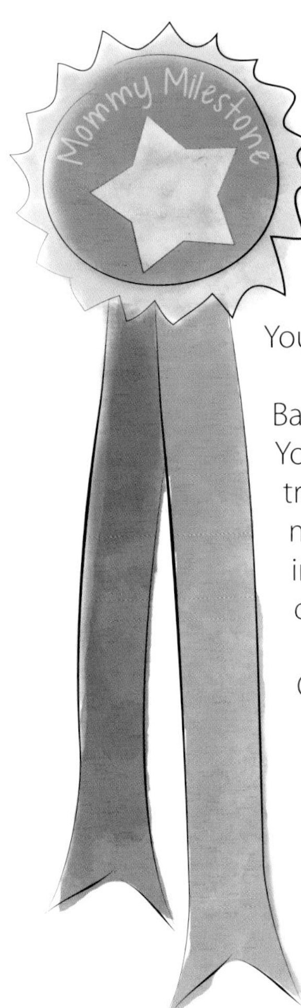

You made it home!

Back in your familiar world, there is a lot to celebrate. You cleared the hospital of your enormous box of treasures, found the car you'd parked days ago, and managed the intricacies of installing a car seat. Finding yourself a bit exhausted and hungry, you totally deserve to nap in your own bed.

Celebrate by ordering dinner in!

My most pressing concern? How to pass my first BM. I had been given vague instructions and suggestions from the nurses and some of my BFFs. But let's be clear: No one lessened the fear factor. I guessed this milestone was something every new mommy faced with nothing short of paralyzing apprehension.

My bathroom shelves now held the unfamiliar. Tucks pads, water spray bottles, cooling creams, and ice packs replaced fragrant candles and fluffy hand towels. For the first time ever, stool softeners appeared on my shopping list. Umm, let's make that

Daddy's shopping list since it seemed only fair that he buy them since *I* had to be the one to take them.

Each time my eyes flitted past the bottle, I cringed. Each uneventful day brought me one step closer to discovering whether those little red pills really did what they claimed. There they sat. Taunting me.

Frankly, the Big Job scared me to death. After childbirth, I assumed pain and injury was behind me. Or, um, beneath me. I didn't want to cause any more damage than had already been done, and *no one* reassured me that the Big Job wouldn't ~~rip me in two~~ land me in the emergency room.

All those non-answers convinced me that if they didn't have something nice to say, they weren't going to say anything at all. Regardless, I was staring down the business end of an unavoidable task.

I worried about my intake of food—and the outcomes of those choices. I steered clear of fiber and oatmeal like the plague. Every morning, I diligently took the stool softener and pretended it was a daily vitamin.

Each time I mounted the porcelain throne, I occupied my mind with a bathroom meditation.

If this is my moment of glory,
please let me be prepared to handle it
without tears,
without tearing,
without another call to Ask-A-Nurse.

With each unproductive attempt, I was granted another day, another reprieve for the part of my body that deserved it the most. Almost a week passed before I felt the urge. I took the position—and my time—and, just like that, everything was fine.

All the prepping and priming, angst and apprehension were for naught. This one milestone had consumed me. Oddly, my husband seemed disinterested in my accomplishment and didn't care to know the details. So, I filled the bathtub and settled for a celebratory soak. Honestly? I hesitated getting serious with the toilet paper. But, hey, let's call it a celebration.

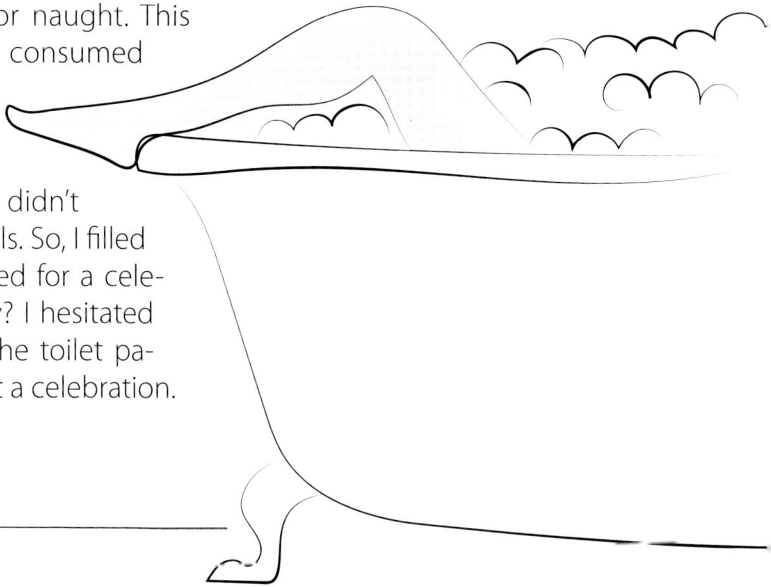

Me: Guess what happened today!

Him: What? Is everything okay?

Remember the thing I have been completely obsessing over?

Umm, only one thing?

You know, about me eventually having to poop?

I think we should be done with this conversation.

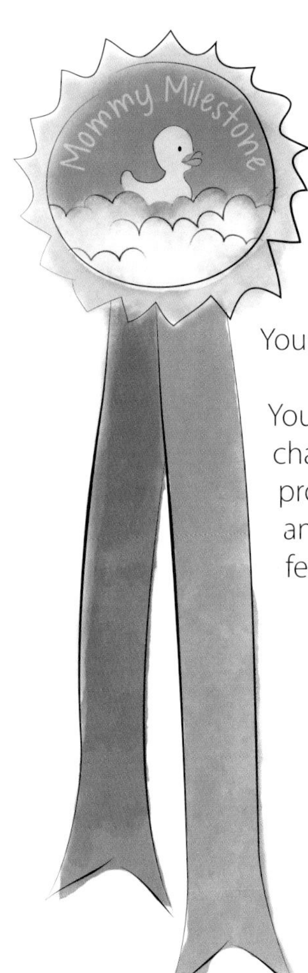

You successfully delivered your first Big Movement!

Your stool softeners came through, you took on the challenge, and you lived to tell about it—though you probably won't squeak a peep to anyone. Go ahead and celebrate. Toss that bottle of stool softeners and fearlessly eat fiber!

Mommy
Milestone
How To
(Almost)
Lose a Nipple
in Seven Days

It was time for the baby's one-week check-up. This was a big day for us, the closest thing to a social event we had experienced since becoming a threesome. Our first excursion as a family.

I was ready to see how far we had come in a week. Not only had I actually showered *and* blow-dried my hair, I applied makeup. Although still using pads both above and below the waist, I managed to trade in my beloved sweatpants for a forgiving skirt. I did the math and had the feedings timed; my babe was full to the brim and wouldn't be hungry again for at least two hours (please and thank you).

The sun was shining, the baby slumbered, and my husband and I became immersed in a quiet conversation about (dare we?) grabbing a bite to eat after the appointment.

We arrived on time (miracle) and picked the softest seat in the waiting room. The baby was measured and weighed, had his temperature taken via tush (deep breath), and passed with flying colors.

Next up: Lactation Consultant. The moment she entered the room, my champion baby delivered an award-worthy portion of his lunch—all over the front of my shirt. Pretending it was nothing (this must happen all the time, right?), I was startled at the tinge of blood in the spit up. The consultant examined the baby's mouth. She paused and looked me in the eyes.

So how is nursing going?

~~I pretty much hate every moment of it~~ Oh, I think I am getting the hang of it.

He is gaining weight and wants to eat every couple hours.

<cue biggest, fakest smile ever seen>

Are you feeling any pain while nursing?

~~The thought of him latching makes me want to cry and I am certain I will never let anyone touch my breasts again~~. Oh, it's a little uncomfortable, but I hear that goes away after a few weeks.

Never good at faking anything (just ask my husband), I knew my smile was weak. The consultant did the unthinkable; she asked to see my poor, aching boobs.

I discretely peeled away a nursing pad. The breast-whisperer confirmed that our little bundle of joy had, in fact, expelled blood on my shirt. No need for alarm. No internal problems on his part. No, the blood came from *me*, from the cracks in my … What?

I looked down and did my own inspection. We spent the next ten minutes practicing exactly what I was trying *not* to do in our off-feeding times.

Latch.

Latch on. Latch off. Rinse and repeat. Experimenting with new positions, rotating the angles. I tried my hardest to mask my pain. Instead, I held my breath and found another use for my Lamaze happy place.

Me: So, that went well?
Him: Umm. Yeah. Sure.
So, did you still want to get something to eat?
Umm. Actually, I've lost my appetite.
Completely understand. Let's go home.

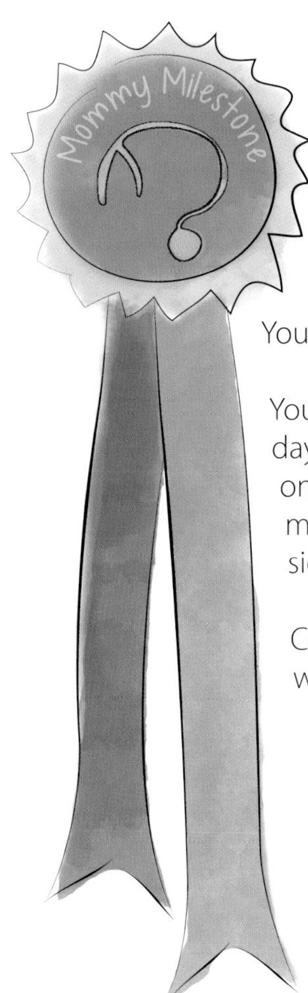

You weathered Week One!

You successfully survived seven nights and seven days with precious little sleep, hardly any routine, and only a vague idea of what date it actually was. You made it to your checkup and proved to the professionals that you are on your way to greatness.

Celebrate by enjoying a feel-good delicious treat that will soothe you from the inside out. You deserve it!

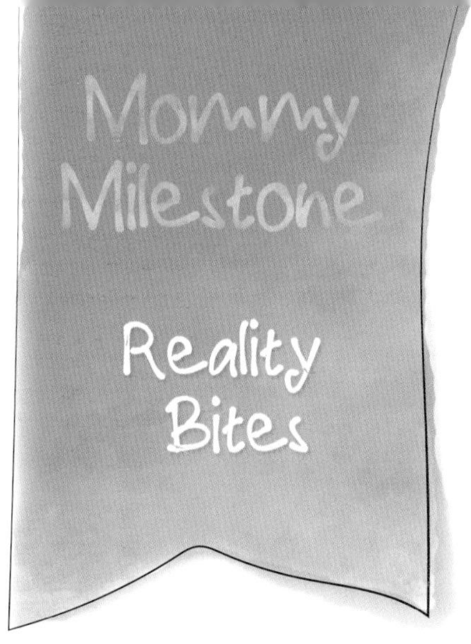

Having my charmed world turn life-changing was like falling into the ocean depths and losing direction. I experienced a chain reaction of constant chaos, sleepless nights, irregular showers, aching bum, and dripping boobs. I hoped for a glimpse of bubbles to indicate which way was up. Instead, I was drowning.

Somewhere between What to Expect and Teaching Baby to Read, I missed the chapter on Basic Survival. Here I thought I would be the mom who easily managed everything thrown her way. Little did I know how much one small person could throw. I knew it was time to ~~drink~~ swim my way back. Survival instincts kicked in, birthing a new attitude that left no room for my former standards and beliefs.

Me: Hello BFF!
BFF: You realize you look a lot better than you smell.
Umm, thanks.
Want to take a minute and go freshen up a bit?
Nope. I'm good. Want some ice cream?

I decided it really didn't matter if the baby slept in my bed, or if I fed him too often, or if I held him nonstop so he wouldn't cry. I wasn't concerned if someone questioned me about his pacifier, how much sleep I was getting, how much ice cream I was consuming. And, let's be clear, the birth announcements weren't out, I hadn't set a date for the baptism, and I had yet to schedule a family photo shoot—let alone sweep the floor when something stuck to my foot.

Judge others? Who, me? What was I thinking?
I should have been taking notes!
I could really use some advice about now.

I wanted to apologize to every mom friend I knew. And I would have. If I'd had the energy.

Dear Mommy Friend,

I am pretty sure this message is long overdue.

I suck. I am sure this isn't news to you.

I need to apologize for my lack of interest in your role as a parent. A lifetime has gone by since I last saw you and your beautiful family. Meanwhile, I became a mom, too. I now realize the responsibilities are incredible and impossible.

I've watched your bustling household, your kids racing around. You. Are. Amazing.

Before now, I had no idea that a new baby brings a priority makeover. If I ever implied you made things too hard, or if I didn't appear to be interested in what you were talking about, I am so sorry. You were gracious to allow a glimpse of your meaningful life, a life full of energy, passion, and sticky door handles.

Thank you for showing me how to embrace this new world, to enjoy the small moments, to not take myself so stinkin' seriously. I look forward to catching up and toasting this awesome role of mommyhood.

Love you dearly

My attitude adjustment was a wake-up call. From this day forward, Plan A was simply whatever would get me through the day. Sinking into the ocean of chaos made me a better person. Sure, I smelled sour and my household would become sticky, but the experience was life-changing (fingers crossed) for the better.

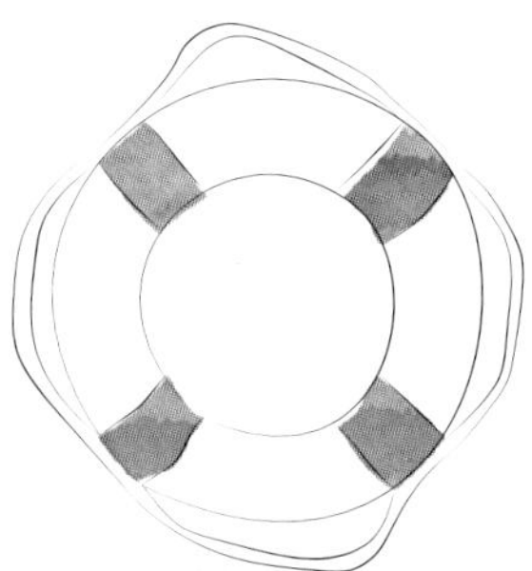

You are discovering your new groove!

Learning what is going to work for *you* is momentous. Sure, perfection sounds nice. But life changes, and sometimes you need to readjust Plan A to Plan Get-through-the-day.

Embrace your newly found discovery and invite over a friend (who is already a member of the Mommy Club) to celebrate your crazy, awesome world!

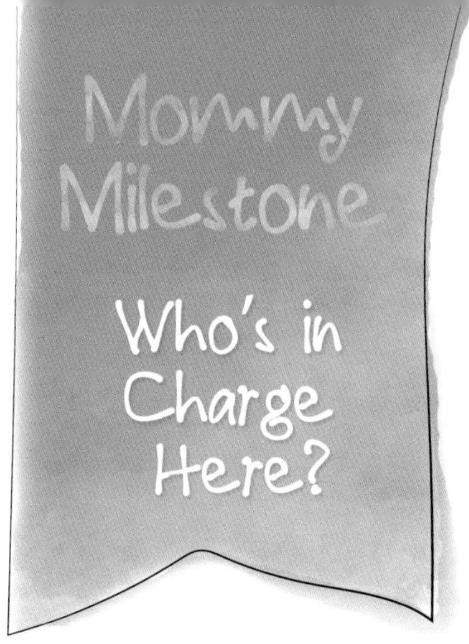

Naturally wired with an optimistic personality, I have a positive outlook and a passion for happy endings. So when I first found out that my maternity leave spanned the entire summer, I thought I'd hit the jackpot. Maybe by week two, I'd feel like going out. Surely I'd have a routine by then. What could be better than an entire summer of relaxing with my bundle of joy?

<enter reality>

For starters, I wasn't up for lakeside barbeques and adult beverages with adult friends. Although I typically looked forward to summer activities, my post-baby body wasn't ready for swimsuit volleyball. Nor was I all that excited to pick up a razor and search for my legs. A quick call to the Ask-A-Nurse Hotline informed me that bug spray and sunscreen weren't for babies under the age of six months. The idea of introducing a sunburnt, mosquito buffet to the neighborhood was all the excuse I needed for the two of us to stay put.

Thanks for the invite.

I'd rather wear sweatpants and stay near the air conditioner.

What I couldn't wrap my mind around was why didn't I *want* to leave my house to enjoy the sunny days and introduce my baby to the world. It drove me crazy. A few thoughts crossed my mind.

Maybe it's because I am sleeping three hours
at a time 'round the clock

or I don't recall the last time I took a shower
and put on makeup

or I am exhausted, sore, still bleeding
(which apparently is completely normal and no reason to
call Ask-A-Nurse for an ETA on the end to this nonsense)

or I look seven months pregnant

or I live in the sweatpants I swore I would burn

or, worse yet, I don't have anywhere pressing to go?

As I sat at the kitchen table perusing my beloved calendar, which ruled my pre-baby world, I started missing my old life. When every moment of my days was planned weeks in advance. When I was important to my team back in the office. When I knew how to cruise through a loaded agenda like a stroll through Candyland.

I thumbed the pages, slightly traumatized to see nothing scheduled for the entire summer season. You'd think tossing the calendar into the closet would've been liberating, a start to the best summer on record. A summer free of office drama, unrealistic timelines, endless unanswered emails.

Instead, I *panicked*. The thought of no one in the outside world needing me for the next three months felt ~~lonesome~~ scary.

As self-administered therapy, I made a list of big-time action items.

To Do List

Pizza
Ice cream
Nursing pads
People Magazine
Diapers
Shower
Call Grandma
Nap
Laundry

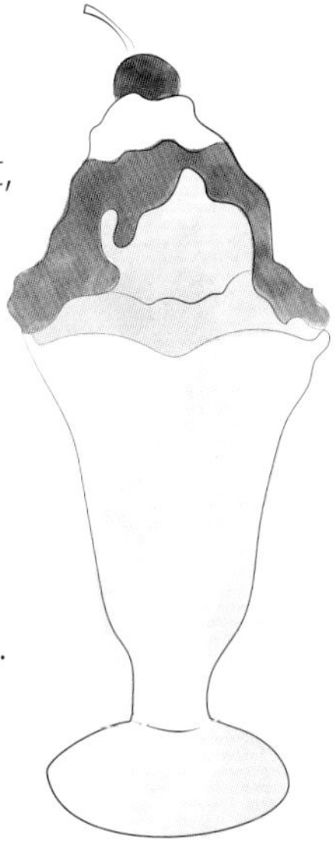

That's when I discovered another milestone moment, recognizing there had been a shift in the organizational chart of the household. I had a new supervisor. A new boss. Anything The Boss needed or cried for? Yup. It was my job to deliver. At times, I found him to be unreasonable.

He didn't adhere to eight-hour workdays.

He ignored my need for coffee and bathroom breaks.

He worked me overtime, both evenings and weekends.

He assured me my job description would never be complete, consistent, or without additional duties as assigned.

My new reality? The Boss never left the office without me by his side. I was on-call for the rest. of. my. life. How long would it take to settle into my new job responsibilities? Even Ask-A-Nurse didn't have the answer to *that* question.

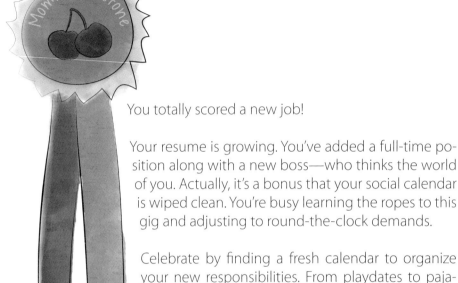

You totally scored a new job!

Your resume is growing. You've added a full-time position along with a new boss—who thinks the world of you. Actually, it's a bonus that your social calendar is wiped clean. You're busy learning the ropes to this gig and adjusting to round-the-clock demands.

Celebrate by finding a fresh calendar to organize your new responsibilities. From playdates to pajama day, movie nights to pizza delivery—enjoy the agenda ahead!

Mommy
Milestone
All You Need
Is Love ...
and a Nap

In my new role, I referenced all the parenting books I had accumulated over the past nine months. Surely I had the resources at my fingertips to grasp this gig, which would pay off nicely with longer periods of sleep, steady weight gain (his, not mine), and the yellow brick road to routine.

As I read the expert advice of seasoned professionals, I started to develop my own ideas about The Boss's fussiness:

Theory 1:
All babies were this fussy behind the scenes and no one warned me.

Theory 2:
He had already been ruined and must be held at all times.

Theory 3:
There was something wrong with him and he needed medical attention.

Armed with assumptions and an arsenal of resources, I threw together the diaper bag, scooped up my blubbering bundle, and raced to the pediatrician's office. Too teary to speak, I handed my book to the doctor and pointed at the paragraph clearly outlining my cause for concern.

BE ALARMED!

1. Crying
2. Spitting up
3. Lack of schedule

I watched the doctor read through my findings, certain he'd be impressed by my developing sixth sense. He reviewed the symptoms and checked the chart. All the while—because and only because I am holding him—*of course* the patient in question slept blissfully, making me look a little ridiculous.

The doctor eyed me over his glasses. He congratulated me on how nicely my son had been gaining weight. He reminded me that all babies spit up and all babies cry and all mothers worry.

Seriously? Is that all the wisdom you can share with me?

~~Sorry for wasting your time.~~ Thanks.

The Boss and I headed home where we met Daddy at the front door. After hearing my story, he promptly boxed up my expert resources, suggesting I not read them for a while. And, with a pinky-promise to steer clear of webMD, I was cut off. Just. like. that.

The next afternoon, I paced a permanent path across our hardwood floor with the screaming, but apparently healthy, Boss. I silently cursed the doctor. I chanted, "Liar, liar, pants on fire!" I dreamed of the day I would hire his first babysitter.

In the midst of my rant and the baby's squalls,
Grandma phoned.

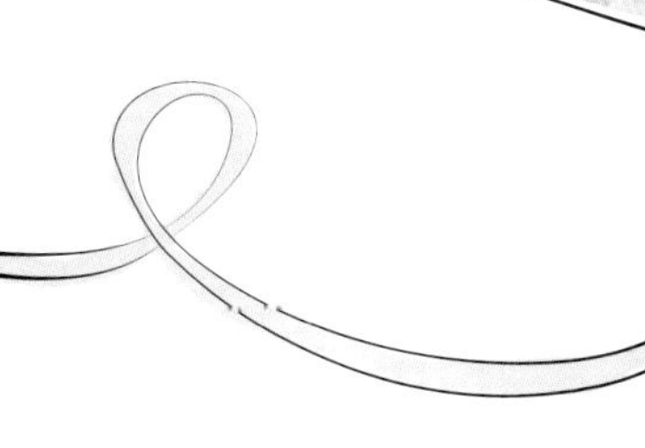

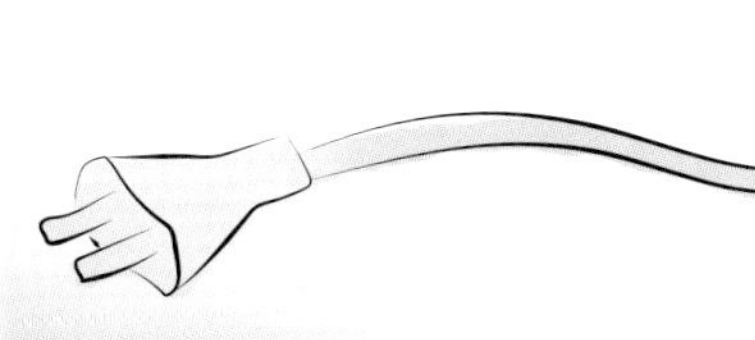

G'ma: What's that I hear? What's the matter with my sweet angel?
Me: I honestly don't know. I even rushed him to the doctor yesterday.
Oh, my. That sounds serious.
It is serious!
Has he eaten?
Check.
Has he pooped?
Check.
Have you taken his temperature?
Trust me. I've covered all the bases. I've tried everything!
What about naps?
A nap? Are you kidding me? I don't have time for a nap!
I meant the baby's naps.
The baby? He isn't interested in taking a nap. He's been up all day!

<cue Grandma freaking out>

After she caught her breath, Grandma ~~lectured~~ explained the importance of naps—for both of us; I'd get mine when The Boss got his. Apparently, infants don't always simply fall asleep; at times, SOMEONE must actually PUT THEM DOWN FOR A NAP. And, yes, she spoke in capital letters.

Okay, so maybe Grandma was on to something.

How had I missed that simple and embarrassingly obvious fact in my research? I blamed it on my exhaustion, my puffiness, my ragged sweatpants. Clearly, naps were so elementary that experts didn't think to remind frantic moms of that critical need. Clearly, experts preferred to list all of the scary alternatives requiring medical attention. And, why hadn't my pediatrician pointed it out? That could have been helpful.

I wonder if webMD would ever consider a
Grandma Knows Best reference?

I approached my drawer full of vital baby gadgets. Gas drops. White-noise machine. Sleep wedge. Wipe warmer. Position pillows. Vibrating chair. And I packed it all away.

Understanding basics is important. So is tapping into Grandma's expertise. Influenced by this gadget-infested world, I needed to be reminded that—back in the day—everything worked out … as long as baby got his nap.

So that mommy got hers, too.

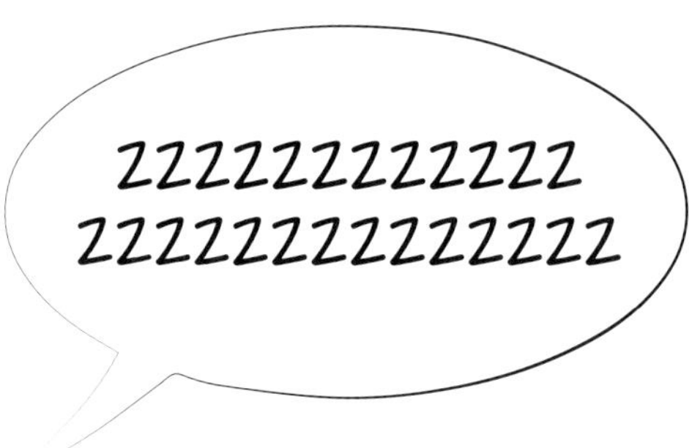

Mommy Milestone

You are learning what you really need!

Quite possibly you have enough information, supplies, and equipment to land on the moon. Although some must-haves are super cute, fuzzy and match the curtains, you are wising up to what is really important. Congratulations on building confidence by trusting your instincts.

Celebrate by taking an hour to clear a shelf of unnecessary items to make room for a few really lovable *wants!*

I finally caved to curiosity. I dared to examine my postpartum body. Whew. It was was time to exercise.

My plan for transformation was simple: I was going to be a Hot Mom. You know what I'm talking about. I intended to be counted among those moms who look amazing, better than before they increased their waist sizes four times the safe-weight gain guidelines.

<Enter Plan A>

With nine weeks of maternity leave remaining, I would be smart about food choices. I would cruise with baby's fancy stroller. I would incorporate those great exercise moves touted in all the mommy magazines. Shedding pounds would be a piece of cake—if I could keep my fork out of it.

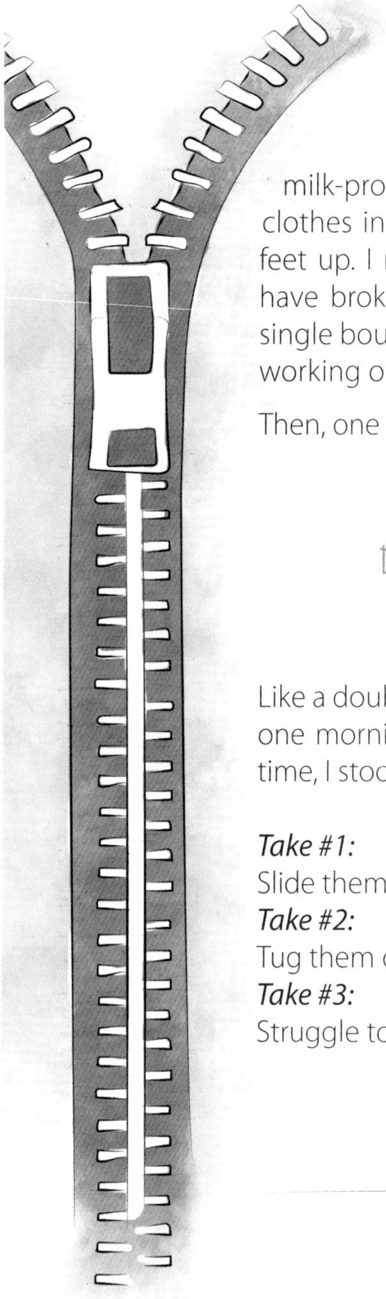

milk-producing glands to slim me back into my zippered clothes in no time. I lunged my way to the couch to put my feet up. I made four trips to unload groceries—when I could have broken my ~~back~~ personal record by carrying them in a single bound. I just knew great results would come from all this working out.

Then, one day, I heard my favorite jeans calling my name.

No elastic waistband. A zipper.
Do I wait until there's a fighting chance?
Or, give it a go?

Like a double-dog-dare, I was drawn to the challenge. First thing one morning, right after I emptied my bladder for the second time, I stood holding my pair of awesome.

Take #1:
Slide them on while standing in front of the mirror.
Take #2:
Tug them on while lying on the bed.
Take #3:
Struggle to the floor and lose any last shreds of dignity.

<cue: curses>

Were these really my favorite jeans?
Maybe I confused them with that small pair?
The ones that fit for one (amazing) summer, only kept to haunt me the rest of my life?

By no stretch of the imagination—or the jeans—could I squeeze myself into them. Deciding I'd faced the zipper challenge two months too soon, I threw up my hands in full surrender … and threw them away.

Favorite, schmavorite.

I went shopping and got myself something new. A flattering skirt with just enough give that no one need worry about being in target range of a strained button.

For the record? I haven't given up on being a Hot Mom. One day, I hope to I find her smiling at me in the mirror.

You have a new relationship with your body!

You've stepped on a scale and looked closely at your body in a mirror. Chances are your image has changed.

Celebrate your sizzling self by rising to a higher level of hot. Shop for a new favorite piece of clothing, one that will make you feel beautiful inside and out.

Outings didn't interest me. The Boss wasn't a huge fan of his car seat and, in general, still cried if I wasn't holding him. At all times.

When we did leave the house, nothing went as planned. The Boss never fell asleep in the car. Ever. Countless friends told how rides lulled their little ones to sleep. Tall tales, if you asked me. Unless I was dangerously close to running out of toilet paper, diapers or ice cream, we stayed put.

No worries little Boss, in twelve short years you can call shotgun.

When the time came for my six-week, post-baby checkup, I made sure Daddy synced his calendar. Not because I wanted him along for moral support. No, I needed him to watch The Boss while I had a heart-to-heart with my ob-gyn. I needed her to tell me where I stood—or at least where I could sit. The doctor would, I envisioned, answer all my burning questions, ultimately confirming that I was a completely normal new mother.

Hence, Daddy took the afternoon shift so I could have my private parts checked out, umm, in private.

I left the house with my purse. That's it. My purse and only my purse. I slid weightlessly into the driver's seat. No diaper bag, no infant carrier. In three seconds flat, I was buckled and ready for takeoff.

Only me.

In my car.

By myself.

No screaming co-pilot to trigger my next move. I could have been in a foreign country, the world felt so different.

The day was colorful, shiny, and bright.
Birds serenaded. Squirrels played tag.
Pansies smiled. Flags fluttered.

Even the radio cooperated by playing my favorite songs. It was the best nineteen blocks I ever drove. Before and since. Clearly I needed more solo time.

I lounged in the waiting room, completely relaxed. I didn't fret about feedings. I didn't have one ear cocked, listening for a cry. Nor was my nose on high alert for a whiff of a blowout. I breezed lazily through a magazine, blissfully carefree.

Carefree and unconcerned that I was about to be weighed in public, said weight recorded permanently in my chart. That I would strip naked, lie in a brightly lit room—spread eagle—and expose my vulnerable areas for review and comment.

I was more relaxed than I had been in six weeks. The nurse called my name and asked me to take my place on the platform.

I slipped out of my shoes and put my purse on the floor,
mentioned that huge glass of water I'd downed,
took off my earrings,
asked the nurse to hold my wedding band.

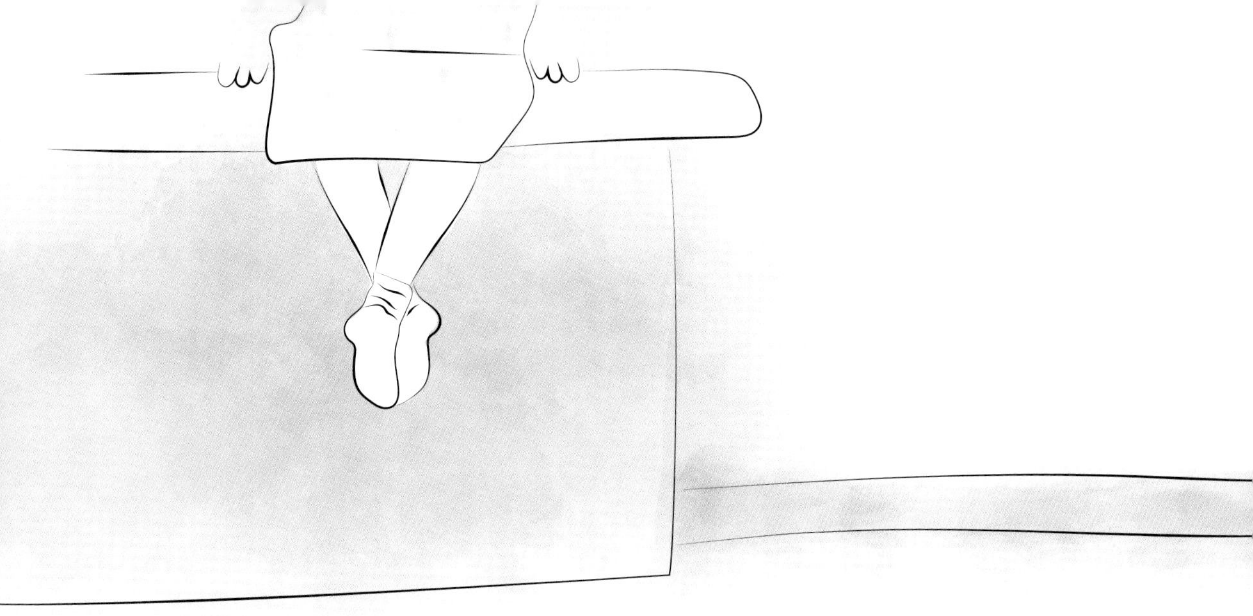

Clearly not interested in becoming fast friends, she escorted me to an examination room where she offered me a ~~napkin~~ sheet to cover myself.

Does it open in the front or the back?
Undies on ... or off?
Can I wear my socks?

Taking my position on the paper lined bed, I shivered and waited. Waited and waited. Was that a new copy of *Parenting*? Sweet. Did I have enough time to grab it off the rack, get back into position, adjust my gown? I decided to go for it.

KNOCK-KNOCK
<door opens>
Hello!

I had a great doctor. Personable, and a mom herself. During the past nine months, we'd gotten to know each other enough to be comfortable, conversational, and honest. After requesting a scootch and a spread, she declared everything satisfactorily healed.

With the lower half of the checkup over, my doctor wrote a prescription for nursing-friendly birth control—which I tucked away so it wouldn't surface for a while—and rolled her chair closer. She asked how I'd been feeling? If I was getting enough rest? How much time was left on my maternity leave? I chirped my answers.

"So," she questioned, "how do you like being a mom?"

And that's when I crumbled.

My eyes flooded. Thoughts about the last six weeks overwhelmed me. Should I tell her how beautiful my baby was? About discovering unconditional love? How much closer I felt to the new daddy? I had all the appropriate answers at my fingertips, yet found myself blurting through a waterfall of tears:

No one told me how much work this was going to be!

She scooted a little closer. "You're spot on. This is the most intense time you will ever know. Being a new mom is hard. But you will find your groove and routine. Your new norm. When you settle into life as a family, the baby won't feel like work. Instead, you'll play, teach, relax, and enjoy."

It was exactly what I needed to hear.

no·pal (nō-'päl, -'pal; 'nō-pəl\, *n.* 1. a fleshy young tender stem segment of the prickly pear cactus. 2. recommended by ask-a-nurse to keep at a safe distance from small children.
nor•mal (nôrməl), *adj.* 1.the usual, average, or typical state or condition
Norn (norn), *n.* 1.any of the three Norse goddesses of fate. 2.a word that is often missed in playdate conversation

Rewarding myself with a decaf latte', I sipped slowly and drove back the nineteen blocks which took the better part of an hour. Don't get me wrong, I kept an eye on the clock as I knew The Boss would be waiting for a snack the moment we were reunited.

I walked into the house and, for the first time, I couldn't wait to see him.

I relieved the shift worker and took my rightful position as #1 Mommy. There was a chance that tomorrow might be easier. Or not. Heck, it could even be worse. After all, the doctor hadn't given me a timeline to get in my groove. But, eventually, I knew I would see motherhood like the gift it really was.

Me: How did it go?

Daddy: We were fine!

Did he miss me? Does he remember me?
Does he even know who I am?

<chirp>

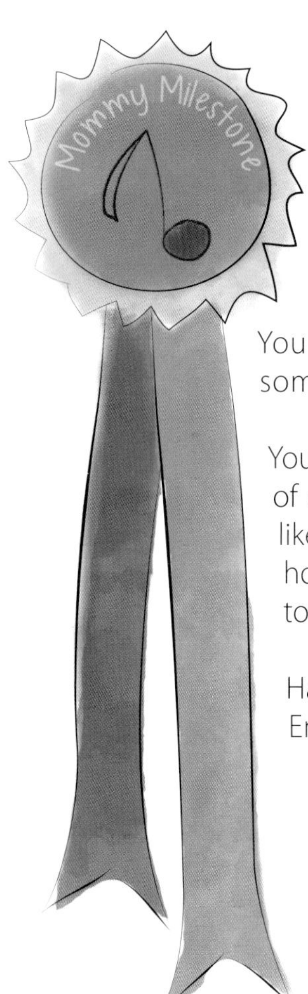

You took a solo road trip and along the way found some reassurance!

You have been attached to baby since the moment of conception and vaguely remember what it was like to venture anywhere by yourself. You can see how your days are going to get easier and that is totally worth celebrating.

Have a latte'. On the house or out of the house. Enjoy every sip.

With our wedding anniversary breathing down my neck, I held an almost-expired gift certificate to our favorite restaurant. Breast milk, squeezed for a special occasion, waited in expectation like the New Years ball, ready to drop. With the planets aligned and all ingredients in place, a night out seemed logical.

Get a sitter. Ditch the sweats.
Dab on mascara. It's a date!

The thought of a ~~night on the town~~ three-hour block of time away from The Boss, both dared and thrilled me. But what about a glass of wine with dinner? For a breast-feeding mom? I had heard of "pumping and dumping"—and thought it ridiculous. Already worried about the milk

I needed to stockpile for returning to work (or not), I couldn't imagine wasting a single drop, even if it was wine-laced.

After drowning in a flood of online information, I decided to call the lactation consultant. I didn't want to give the professional the wrong idea of my drinking intentions—I mean, she didn't even know me, but certainly I wanted to be responsible and enjoy my night out to the best of my ability.

Me: Our anniversary is coming up and we're planning a date night. I wanted to double check the guidelines for wine with dinner?

Consultant: It takes two hours to remove one glass of wine from your system.

What if I drink two glasses of wine in the first hour of dinner? How long before I can nurse?

Two drinks at two hours each? That would be four hours.

Really?

Yes.

But we were going to be out for three hours. Did I mention it was our anniversary? Maybe I forgot to mention I have a gift certificate? Does it matter that we haven't been out yet since The Boss moved in?

It takes two hours to remove one glass of wine from your system.

Clearly she doesn't understand my question.

Maybe I need to speak slower? Louder?

Maybe I should hang up and redial hoping for a different perspective?

So I can have one glass of wine with dinner. Regardless of how quickly I drink it. Regardless of what kind it is. Regardless of how much fun I am having. Regardless of it being our anniversary and we have a gift certificate. Got it. One glass, two hours to safely nurse The Boss when I get home. You have been super helpful and clear.

You're welcome. Happy anniversary.

We packed everything The Boss could possibly need and arrived at the home of a trusted aunt. As I talked through a number of scenarios, I noticed she wasn't taking any notes and recalled that she had four adult children and a lapful of grandkids. She already knew her way around the baby block.

<cue moving right along>

So there we were, Mommy and Daddy, alone. What would we talk about? Something other than baby, of course. There were, after all, other things to discuss, to focus on. Right?

How are those cracked nipples?

Does the lactation consultant
think you have a drinking problem?

Wanna talk about the sex we haven't had yet?

<enter small talk>

"What a gorgeous restaurant."

"What a beautiful painting on the wall."

"What should we order?"

That coveted night reminded us that we were *first a couple* and, now, parents. Our experiences over the past nine weeks had pushed boundaries in ways we couldn't have imagined. Sleepless nights and never-ending interruptions made us exhausted and grumpy, yet somehow molded us into better people. We began to discuss how much we appreciated each other for what we were both going through. We laughed at how memorable some of the moments had been … and how some we'd like to forget.

The evening's heartfelt conversation focused on us. Us, prioritizing time for each other. Us, inventing crazy, fun ways to enjoy our new family. Us, dreaming about our first vacation (once I wasn't limited to one ~~measly~~ glass of wine).

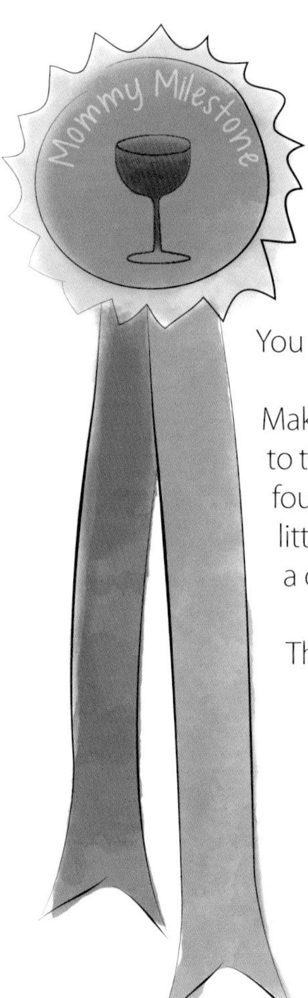

You went out on a first date with a guy named Daddy!

Making arrangements so you can re-introduce yourself to the special someone in your life is *so full of good*. You found something to talk about other than your new little person and managed to spend quality time as a couple.

This milestone *is* the celebration. Cheers!

Photos taken during our early days home from the hospital captured a ~~nasty~~ pattern with my appearance. Hair scooped into a ponytail, just moments out of the shower (or not), was a style hard to beat. Tidy and out of the way—what's not to love? I'm not sayin' my new do was trending in the fashion mags, and, yes, wet and shiny *might* be mistaken for greasy through a camera lens. And, I admit, it wasn't the look I aspired to. Even so, easy and fast fit my not-going-anywhere-soon lifestyle.

As time passed, I eased back into the groove of proper self-maintenance, thanks to invaluable advice from a distant cousin.

"The baby cannot hurt himself in the crib," she assured me. "He will be absolutely fine while you get ready."

Daddy: Could you mention something to the beautiful new mommy about taking some time for herself?
Brilliant Cousin: Are you wanting me to mention she should do something with her hair?
You're reading my mind!

I had a hunch Daddy had something to do with the much needed advice.

A week into my new hygiene routine, I discovered that the shower drain wasn't keeping up with the water flow. It was time to bring Daddy in for a look. He lugged his macho toolbox up the stairs to explore the problem—and I was wise enough to get out of his way. I'd wait to hear his victory yell.

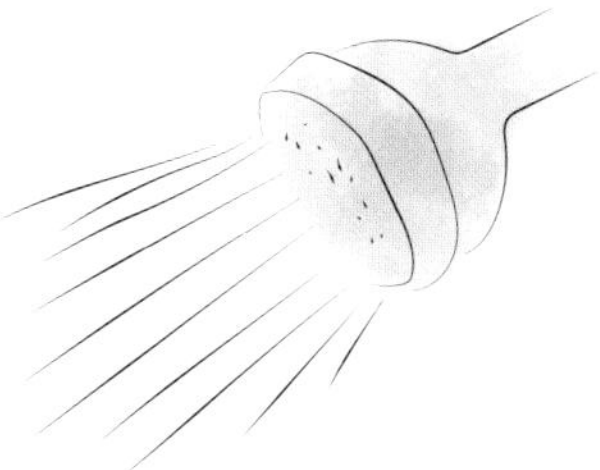

But I did wonder why the drain was sluggish. I mean, The Boss certainly wasn't doing anything that I didn't know about (yet). And I hadn't been shaving ~~at all~~ much, so that certainly wasn't an issue.

I waited. And waited.

A manly shriek of pure horror came from the bathroom. From the drain, he'd pulled a blonde hairball worthy of any massive feline.

Him: Is there any hair left on your head?

Me: Umm, last time I checked.

This is disgusting.

Really?

You think that is disgusting?

Totally.

Oh, so you think you know disgusting? Have you ever had to clip off skin tags that appear for no reason? Have you ever had your skin pulled so tight it caused stretch marks that might not ever go away? Have you ever even heard of cankles? Seriously, a little hair (ok maybe a lot) in a drain is all you can take? Pull it together, Sweetheart. I am the one going bald!

Ugh. Got it.

And, just like that, in one ranting moment, all of the new discoveries I was trying to keep on the down-low from everyone (especially the resident plumber) were bared to the world.

I scurried to the phone to ask a mommy friend why the topic of wig shopping hadn't risen in any of our what-to-expect conversations. Of course she thought I was overreacting and asked whether I remembered her being bald.

I took a calming breath. Okay. Fair enough.

My panic diminished to a keep-an-eye-on-it strategy. The activity found growing on—and falling off—my body, then adding all that spewed and dripped from The Boss … I realized I could handle the load, after all.

But lesson learned, I would keep it to myself from now on.

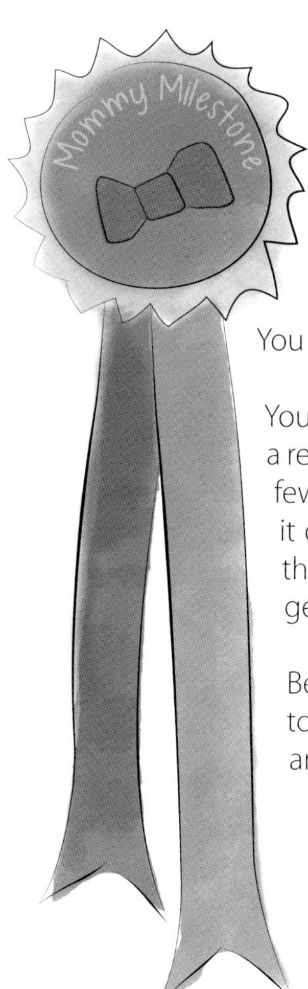

You aren't going bald anytime soon!

Your body is trying to regain balance, but patience is a requirement. The good news: You have discovered a few tricks to streamline your morning primping, and it definitely looks good on you. You actually passed this milestone and still have your hair. But don't forget to thank your household plumber.

Be sure to celebrate by taking a well-deserved trip to the salon for a little self-pampering. Your fingers and toes will be grateful for the attention!

Mommy
Milestone
So Much
to Do,
So Little Time
to Shower

Pre-mommyhood, I was organized, productive, and a magnet for social outings. I divided my days into thirty-minute increments and prioritized and juggled activities with the best of the best.

Now my days blurred, a vicious circle of feed and nap, feed and diapers, rinse and repeat. For the first time in my adult life, I struggled to remember the day of the week, let alone the year. An excellent excuse, I reasoned, to watch the "Today Show"—just to keep me on track. I longed for a schedule. Or at least a paper trail to prove what I had accomplished lately.

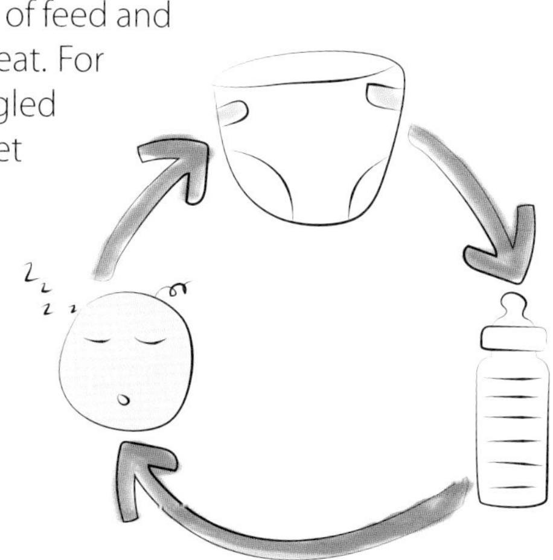

I became smitten with a month-at-a-glance calendar that allowed me one square space per day. It was a beautiful thing, a record of my days. Writing "call mom" in one of those sweet spaces resulted in a heady rush of accomplishment. Notes like "laundry" or "diaper run" filled the squares and proved—in ink—the fullness of my days. In fact, a bath for The Boss and a shower for me should be considered a full day in any mommy's book.

I knew many moms cruised through this stage without so much as a blink of an eye. They phoned from time to time to schedule a mommy-baby date, only to find their calendars filled.

Ambitious Mom: We'd love to meet your new addition!

Me: Maybe tomorrow for coffee?

Sorry, I'm booked. Another day?

How about Wednesday?

No good. Yoga and lunch plans. Another day?

You tell me when you have thirty minutes to squeeze us in.

I came up with a few ideas that could be factors with my activity level:

1. My maternity leave was limited and soon my sweatpants would be out of style. Was it really necessary to be out and about?
2. Maybe strangers wouldn't mind listening to The Boss scream. Should I widen my comfort zone?
3. Maybe my mommy-friends' crammed calendars were mere sham. Had I fallen for their charades?
4. Was I simply content, too ~~lazy~~ comfortable to leave?

Honestly? I was satisfied with a one-activity-a-day pace. A single action item made me feel productive. Leaving the house twice in the same day seemed wildly extravagant and equally unnecessary. Perfect thinking, I concluded, since the local grocery store just started offering new services: online ordering and home delivery.

Would a hefty tip convince them to stop by the coffee shop and pick up a large latte for me?

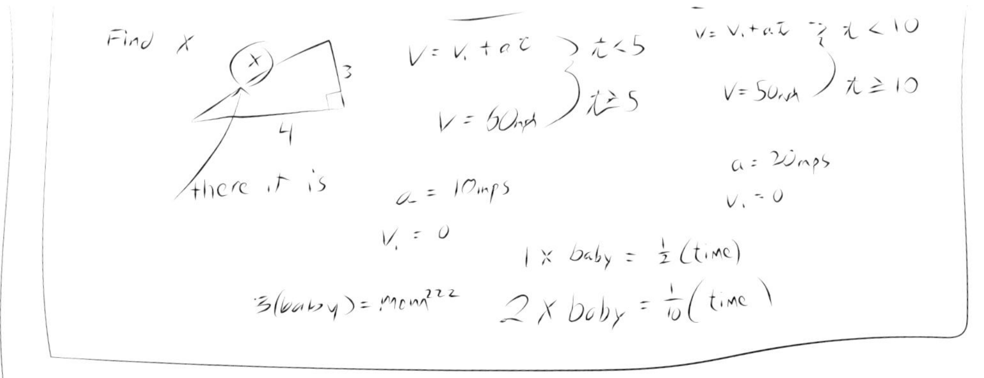

The need to arrive anywhere on time consumed me; I considered the minute details of all appointments days ahead of time. Leaving the house required a mathematic skill-set worthy of high school algebra.

The Problem:

Your baby eats at 7:20 a.m. The doctor expects you at 11:15 a.m. Arrive fifteen minutes early to check in. Before leaving the house, you must: shower, brush your teeth (not optional), do your hair and apply makeup (optional), pack a diaper bag, and change three diapers.

***Additional information that may or may not be relevant*:**

History proves you are capable of settling into the car in 12 minutes, but can take up to 20 minutes (if you notice a foul odor emanating from the baby). Additional consideration must be given to possible en route blowouts. Speed limits in your city are 25mph. You live 8 miles from the doctor's office.

The Questions:

1. At what time does your car need to leave the driveway to make it to the appointment on time?
2. How many diaper changes are necessary in that time frame and how many diapers should be packed?
3. What time do you need to exit the building post-appointment to avoid the scene of a screaming hungry baby?
4. What are the odds that you will actually take a shower?
5. Extra credit: Which side will you nurse on when you return home?

To be clear, I wasn't at the head of my class. But, after a few botched attempts, my brain calculated at Mach speed to determine whether Train A or Train B would get us to the appointment on time. Fed *and* freshly diapered.

My high school math teacher would be proud.
Cheers to you, Mr. Overby.

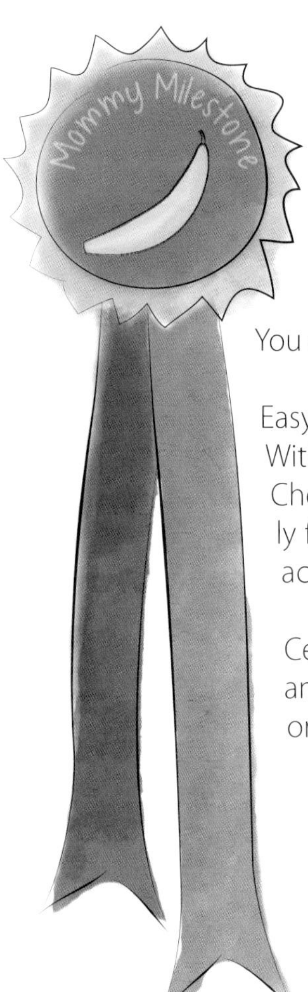

You are learning how to schedule your time!

Easy or not, understanding your limits is a big deal. With so much going on in your world, be selective. Choose your outings with care and arrive in a timely fashion. Knowing your comfort level of add-on activities is a step in the right direction.

Celebrate by scheduling a perfect day for yourself and your baby. Elaborate or low-key, venturing out or keeping cozy. You decide and enjoy!

Mommy Milestone
On My Honor, I Promise to Buy TP

I was excited to spend the afternoon at ~~the Emerald City~~ Target. Not yet having the luxury of a leisurely shopping excursion, I qualified as being dangerously close to an emergency situation; toilet paper and toothpaste were nearly extinct in my house.

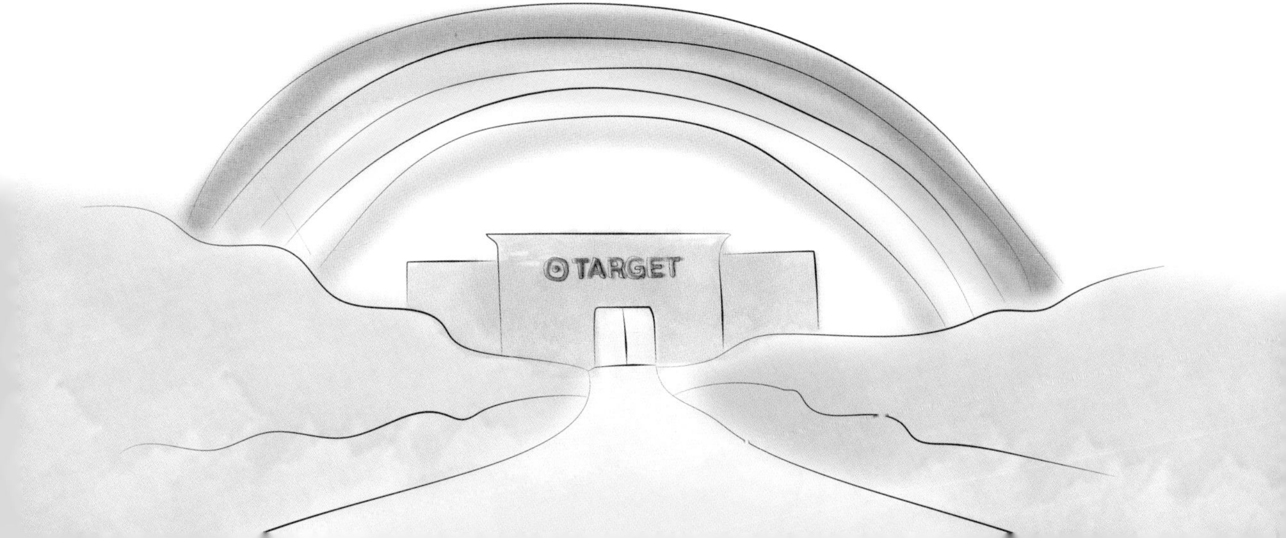

I bundled The Boss and we were off for the adventure of the day. We didn't need to accommodate anyone's schedule but our own. I factored a solid one-and-half hours to dilly-dally through the aisles on a random weekday, while my recently fed co-pilot napped blissfully in his carrier.

The Boss was bright-eyed, impressed with the shopping palace. He felt the good vibes shooting from every pore of my body. We were at the place where happiness—or the closest thing to it—*could* be bought … in the shape of one-size-fits-most socks. I couldn't wait to fill my cart with can't-live-without items that I was certain would make our lives easier and more colorful. Five minutes into our spree, I was stopped by a sweet lady who praised my beautiful baby.

The Boss played it up, charming her with his sparkling eyes and shimmery, drooling lips. I glowed and gushed.

Why am I rambling to a total stranger?
And why is she even remotely interested?

She told me all about her family and how she anticipated grand-kids. The next thing I knew, I found myself looking at family photos and recent wedding proofs, wishing with her that they all lived a little closer to one another.

AHEM:

You are getting caught up in this lady's life.

Tick-Tock-Tick-Tock.

Twenty minutes of your leisurely shopping excursion, gone.

I scooted to the baby aisles and found myself in the diaper section, making eye contact with a soon-to-be new mommy. Understandably, she was smitten by The Boss, who was oh-so-close to drifting off—only to be startled when she oohed and ahhed over him. *Of course* I needed to ask her the details of her impending due date (no option on this one) and quickly found she was full of questions for me. I tried to sound somewhat knowledgeable, but Daddy was clearly the Consumer Reports analyst in our household.

Adorable Preggie: Any advice on the type of bottles?

Me: Umm, that's a good question. You are going to be a great mom!

How about diapers? Any advice?

You will definitely need lots of those. Oh, you mean the brand? Umm.

What about little socks and washcloths? Are they really necessary?

I know we own them. How would you define "necessary?"

With all our jibber-jabber, The Boss got restless. Stunned at the racing clock and the lack of treasures in my cart, I knew it was time to step up the pace.

As we rolled along, I noticed eyes dissecting me. I surreptitiously checked my zipper. I patted my chest for leaks. If those eyes weren't on me before, they certainly found their way to the mommy who just felt herself up.

ATTENTION SHOPPERS: Eyes to yourself!

At that moment, an elderly couple changed lanes to peek at my perfect passenger.

As the sweet couple told me all about their own grandkids, my nose caught a whiff of ripe diaper. Unbelievable. My last minutes of what should have been a zen experience were ending with a stinky butt? Without me even catching a glimpse of what *wasn't* going home with me?

Doesn't anyone work anymore?
Why are so many people shopping smack in the middle of the week?
Wait ... wait. What day is it, anyway?

Outings with The Boss, I learned, were priceless yet time-consuming. I found it impossible to ignore any conversation that started with, "Your baby is adorable."

Fair warning: No matter the clock, no matter the admiration, no matter the leak you find on your shirt … don't even think about leaving the store without buying toilet paper.

Mommy Milestone

You are a magnet for compliments!

Introducing your baby to the world can be thrilling, even a bit overwhelming. You are more eye-catching than a celebrity sighting and have learned your baby is the surest way to start a conversation with complete strangers.

Celebrate your popularity by taking a moment to enjoy the traffic-stopping attention you gather because, yes, you both are that awesome!

Mommy Milestone
Over the River and Through the Woods

There comes a time when you feel pressured to leave your cozy nest and spend the weekend away with loved ones. As exciting as it was to introduce The Boss to my hometown, the thought of being in a world that ran on a full night's sleep made me ~~terrified~~ nervous. But, hey, they were my parents for crying out loud. Parents who raised four girls and now had a bustling houseful of grandkids. It was time to get over it and pack the car already.

G'ma: I bet he is getting so big.

Me: Sure is. Amazing how fast they grow.

It would be wonderful to see you all.

You can stop by anytime. Please call first.

You should come for the weekend.

Oh, I am sure you guys are busy.

We are wide open.

Is that so ...

Perfect. I can't wait! Come in time for dinner.

Umm ... great. New Daddy will be so excited.

It took me an entire day to pack the supplies I thought I needed for The Boss (and me).

What am I going to wear?

I was certain Grandma wasn't going to be impressed with the sweatpants I sported every time she visited. I reluctantly pulled out my nicest *early* maternity clothes in hopes no one would recognize them. Which they shouldn't. I'd hardly worn them. The label might as well have read: ~~*SUCKER*~~ *First-timer who doesn't know how enormous you'll eventually be.*

His tummy was filled to the max, his must-haves were packed neatly in the car, and his nap was aligned perfectly with the one-hour-and-twenty-minute car ride to Grandma's house. The Boss was ready for departure, just in time for Daddy to navigate our maiden voyage.

We were barely outside of town when the pacifier—tucked snuggly into his mouth—plunged into the hopeless abyss of the floor. And so began the longest car ride of our lives.

Rear-facing, The Boss wasn't interested in listening to me sing, soothe, or tell jokes. Nope. He was as angry with me as I was with my inability to rotate my elbow 360 degrees. After forty-five minutes of screaming (him, not me), I made the decision to save our ~~marriage~~ sanity. I unbelted myself and crawled into the back seat, searching frantically for the Holy Grail.

By now, The Boss was so worked up that it didn't take him long to fall asleep. In the sudden stillness, I was terrified to make a peep, so we rode in absolute silence the remainder of the trip—holding our breaths over every bump in the road.

We arrived.

Grandma and Grandpa raced to greet us with open arms. Meanwhile, I desperately needed to use the bathroom, Daddy needed to unpack the car, and The Boss needed a diaper change. So Grandma needed to sit tight and wait for the maintenance to take place before she could have her way with us all.

Once settled into our weekend residence, we found ourselves enjoying the relaxing environment, complete with all-inclusive, five-star treatment. And it only got better with snacks, refreshing drinks, and the tantalizing aroma of dinner simmering in the oven.

Me: You really outdid yourself, Grandma. This is delicious.

G'ma: So glad you like it. It's the same old recipe you've eaten a thousand times.

Unbelievable. What do you call it?

Hamburger Hot Dish.

Huh. Surprising the difference eating it hot makes. Is there dessert?

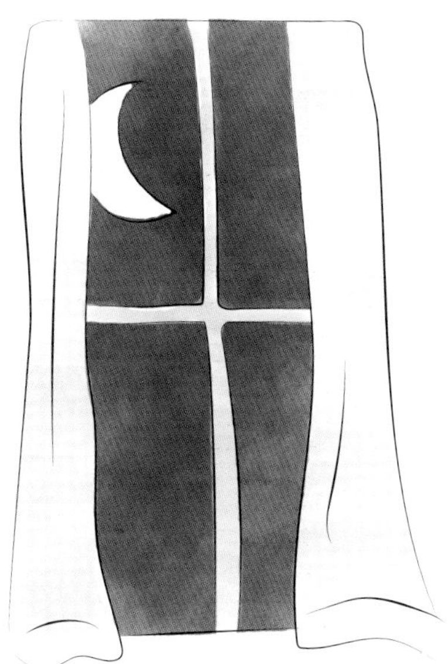

Life was good.

Dessert was even better.

<cue bedtime>

Lights were turning off throughout the house—a subtle hint that the day had come to an end. But we had a little secret that, like it or not, was about to become public knowledge: We. Had. No. Routine. Bedtime was impossible, and the challenge was now staring us in the sleepy face.

I felt the pressing need to come up with reasons our angel wasn't cooperating: We had a traumatic drive, literally the longest in The Boss' life. We were in a new environment: new bed, new people, new smells. His sleep pattern was off due to a scream-induced nap in the car.

Oh, I had some good excuses, but—relying on his track record—I knew The Boss wasn't going to drift off anytime soon.

It was time to get my A-game on:

Strategy #1: Pacing
Walking, walking, and more walking. Thirty minutes turned into sixty, that turned into madness, and we were all still wide awake and getting a little crabby.

Strategy #2: Swaddling
Rolling him up burrito-tight, laying him down, and soothing. It'd never worked before, but what the heck, maybe Grandma's house had magical powers to make this time different. Or not.

Strategy #3: Feeding
Time to play dirty and pull out the warm milk, even though he ate just before we started this terror.

Long hours later, we finally scored and, lucky for us, in a few short winks it would be time to start the day all over again.

<enter sunshine>

Breakfast was delicious and, not surprisingly, the topic of routine wriggled and squirmed its way into our conversation. I suffered through the helpful tips, agreeing with anything and everything offered. After all, I wasn't anti-routine; I was clueless how to get one.

AGREED: We haven't established a routine (not even close).
AGREED: We don't have any control of our situation.
AGREED: We need to work on that.

Could you please pass the coffee and another caramel roll?
Yawn.
What were we talking about?

I learned to drink coffee while sleeping with my eyes open that morning.

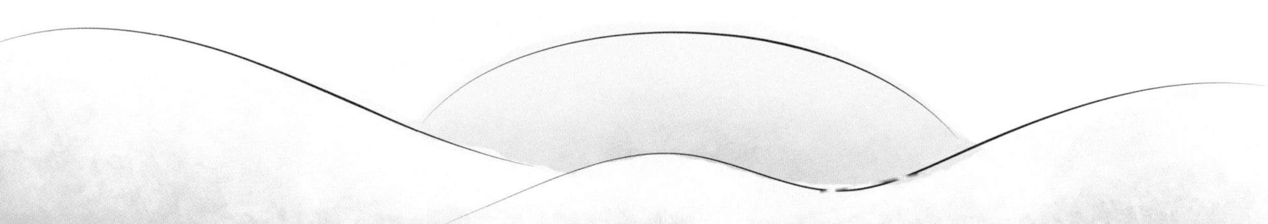

Hello!
My name is
Mommy

We made it to church on time, a miracle in itself, and wouldn't you know it, The Boss slept through the whole thing. Angel. Yep, that's my angel.

A slew of family and old friends met our little one that day. And they met a new me.

That's right. Responsible for another human being now, I would never again be the same me. It felt wildly natural to bring conversations to a different level with these people, people who had known me my whole life. We didn't talk about the current events of our small town; instead we discussed the magic new life brings.

What did we ever talk about pre-baby?
My hair? My job?
My lack of interesting things to talk about?

Being in a group of familiar faces with a fresh perspective was incredible. Laughing, sympathizing, understanding we weren't alone on our journeys and how we each had reached milestones brought us closer. I may have felt isolated at 3:00 a.m. the night before, but the reward was being able to share moments with those I loved. It was the cherry on top.

You went on an overnight adventure!

So much can happen when you allow yourself to wade into the big world. You find challenges and opportunities at every turn. Good or bad, you learn, grow and—hopefully—get a hot meal out of the deal.

Extend your bravery and expand your world just a bit more. Join a local group or plan a trip, solo or with the family. You pick!

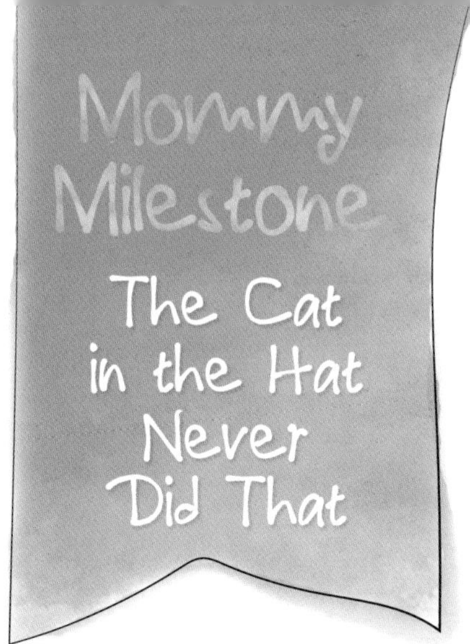

Mommy Milestone
The Cat in the Hat Never Did That

Someone, somewhere, came up with the notion that six weeks after giving birth a gal is ready for a little serving of "shimmy shimmy cocoa puff"—but I had a couple of notions of my own.

Theory #1:
In a conference room many, many moons ago, a group of male doctors made a pact, spun around three times, spit in their hands, and shook on the deal.

Theory #2:
Way back before women had the right to vote, a grand lobbying effort placed the timeline for post-baby sex on the ballot. It passed.

I understood that new daddies in every corner of the world had their wives' A-okay exam circled on their calendars. And not so they could greet them at the door afterwards with ice cream.

At my post-baby checkup, the topic of bringing sexy back headed the agenda.

Doc: You did a nice job healing.

Me: Thank you. I guess I tried my best.

You are set to resume all regular activity.

What exactly do you mean?

You are ready for your regular activities.

So you think I can toss the squirt bottle and join a gym?

You can toss the squirt bottle—and have sex.

You aren't going to tell anyone. Right?

I'll let you share the good news when you're ready.

Perfect.

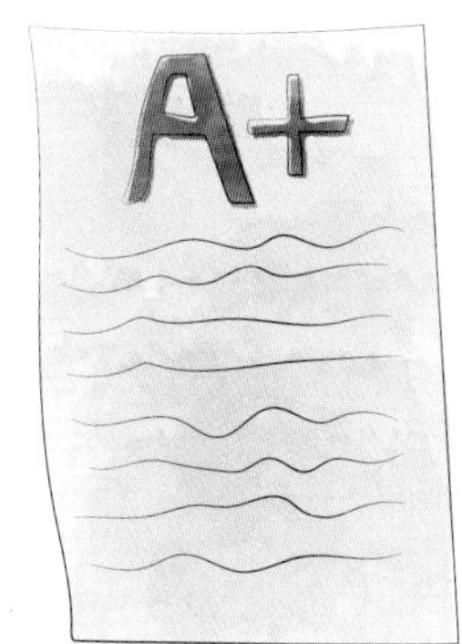

I wasn't eager to post my A+ vagina report card on the refrigerator. My thoughts raced. Exactly how sexy did a new mommy need to feel before steaming up the windows? Daddy wouldn't need much to get in the mood, but for crying out loud, it'd been six ~~short~~ *weeks!*

I hadn't begun to lose any weight. I couldn't recall the last time I shaved any part of my body. My boobs leaked from time to time. Totally random.

A team player, I realized I needed to come up with a game plan to help me prepare for The Big Dance.

Sextuplet [seks-tuhp-lit] n. 1. a group or combination of six things. 2. typically not a word you want to hear at your ultrasound.

sex·y [sek-see] adj, sex·i·er, sex·i·est. 1. concerned predominantly or excessively with sex 2. sexually interesting or exciting

Seymour [se(y)-mour] n. 1. Jane, c1510–37, third wife of Henry VIII of England and mother of Edward VI. 2. not a popular name for baby boys 3. see more what?

What to wear?
The easy answer according to new Daddy: nothing.

This wasn't how I was going to roll. Nothing on top while my boobs dripped was not an option. They needed comfortable and forgiving support. Let it be known that those fixtures were off limits. No exceptions.

Would everything work?
My doctor suggested I purchase some slippery assistance. This dance, she warned, would be different from the last dance. Not that I could remember when that was. I added a tube of slippery to *my* grocery list, because this errand for Daddy would establish expectations for the evening's not tonight agenda.

What is the plan?
We were on borrowed time and at the mercy of The Boss. One shout-out from him would conclude our interlude. Regardless of dance position, or how awesome we thought we were, the odds of warming back up anytime soon wouldn't be probable. Focus on the business at hand, we determined; get in and get out.

<many weeks later>

We did it. I wouldn't describe it as amazing, but it was good. Good to connect. Good to be over.

You had sex for the first time as a mommy!

This is a big day for you and your partner - congratulations on jumping back into the sheets! You might have been excited, nervous, terrified, and quite possibly all of the above. It's crazy important to find ways to connect both in and out of the bedroom and to remember just how good it feels to share special moments with each other.

Celebrate your sexy self by trading in your shabby tee shirt and scrub pants for new sleepwear. Lace or fleece, one piece or two, anything goes as long as it fits your sass when the mood hits!

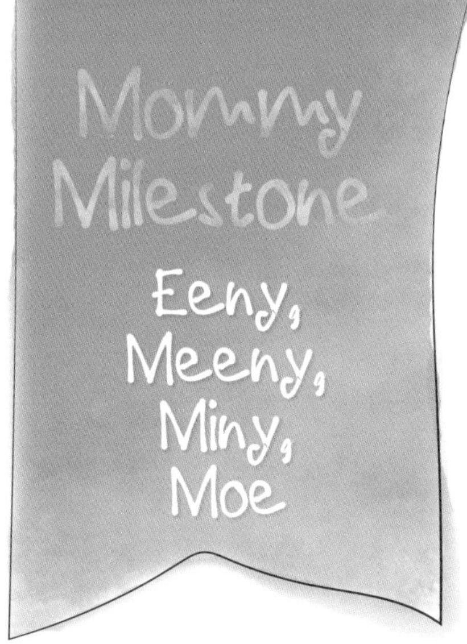

Questions regarding maternity leave plans arose long before the baby arrived.

When are you due?

Is this your first baby?

Should you be eating that?

What are you having?

The length of my maternity leave was a hot topic. Possibly, my coworkers worried they'd never see me again. Give me a break people: I hadn't even pushed this baby into the world, and already I was pondering when I'd return to work.

I was blessed to have the option of a three-month hiatus which—when flipping pages in a weekly calendar—looked like a lifetime, a lifetime filled with opportunities galore. Free time, Baby, and lots of it. Maternity leave would be the most productive phase of my life.

I will start an exercise plan and get back into my jeans!
I will catch up all my correspondence!
I will organize the entire house!
I will clean out all my closets!
I will learn how to cook!

And, in the blink of an eye, it was time to make the decision. Go back to work? Stay home?

Some decisions, I knew, were made by purely gut feelings. But others were made by the reality of the resources available. My situation was a mix, and I started to prep for returning to the office.

I stood in the kitchen in my stretchy pants and looked around my disorganized house, realizing just how off-target my expectations had been. And, you'd be correct if you guessed I hadn't written many letters in the past few weeks—unless panicked phone calls for Grandma's advice counted as thinking-of-you communication. I promise I had good intentions.

"Oh, look at this beautiful Thank You for Being a Great Role Model card I got today," said no grandma. Ever.

The end of maternity leave brought an end to many things I had grown to love. Bonding with The Boss was amazing. We solved life's mysteries in the rocking chair, relished playdates in the middle of the week with new friends and thrived on countless naps, cuddled on the couch. Our uninterrupted time was ~~exhausting~~ priceless, and I knew the memories would last a lifetime.

But let's not forget my newly found love for loungewear. And my disregard for calendars. Oddly, I'd adjusted to getting up three times a night for warm milk (for him) and cookies (for me). Quick study that I was, I had caught on to a rhythm of napping when he napped, eating when he ate. Sure, we had some rough patches, but we made it—thanks to the Ask-A-Nurse Hotline.

All too soon, The Day arrived. And it began at 8:00. In the morning.

That's not jewelry. That's drool.

I was expected to look presentable. To wear clothes that didn't coordinate with tennis shoes. To arrive on time. To be productive all. day. long.

Daddy pushed me out the door in the nick of time. My first step into my next adventure—and the longest day *ever* for a new mommy.

Mommy Milestone

You made a huge decision for your new reality!

Deciding to be a stay-at-home or a working-else-where mommy is a big moment. No right or wrong, only time to congratulate yourself on an emotional decision. Stop second-guessing your choice and start enjoying your path.

Build a little self-renewal into your routine. Make time to put your feet up, get lost in a book or magazine, meet a friend for coffee, or take a solo walk—gifts only you can give yourself.

Believe it or not, while you're on maternity leave, the rest of the world continues to do business in the same manner as always. Without you. Although I'd worked harder than ever during the past twelve weeks for Little Boss, there was another boss in my life (but not as cute or as cuddly) waiting for me to clock in.

It was a crazy day. I dropped off my most prized possession to trusted childcare professionals and *left* him there. Walking out the door empty-handed, fingers crossed, I hoped I was doing the right thing. With a few tears shed in the car, I pulled away on the next leg of my big adventure.

Surprisingly, (and thankfully) the familiar routine at work felt right. I was amazed at how productive I could be in an environment where I could use *both* hands without playing defense with The Boss. Er, the Little Boss, that is. I was back—and determined to be awesome.

Committed to do it all, I continued my efforts to provide liquid gold. Armed with my pump, ready for action, I tackled the "nursing talk," a milestone in itself.

Big Boss: Welcome back! It's a jam-packed, full-throttle day!

Me: Thanks. But, about that jam-packed part? I need a thirty minute break in the morning as well as ...

And your calendar is crammed with catch-you-up-to-speed meetings and ...

... a thirty minute break in the afternoon to, uh ...

... the team is excited to take you to lunch to celebrate ... Uh, breaks? Today?

Well, every day.

Anything I should be concerned about?

No. To continue breastfeeding, I'll need to pump twice each day.

Er, good for you.

Let me know if you have any questions.

<silence>

Well, then, great. Thanks for your support!

I made it painfully clear to all who walked the halls that if my office door was closed, it was not to be opened. Ever.

If the building was in flames, I didn't care to know.

If Bono, himself, was there to see me, he would have to wait.

I'd heard the stories, stories about nursing mommies using office closets, restrooms, storage rooms. Locked doors were a luxury. Encountering the company janitor exposed (me, not him) would mean looking for a new job (again me, not him), no doubt about it. I was grateful to have a private space where I could support my moonlighting gig in the production industry.

It was time to tune out the noise of office, coworkers, and photocopiers. It was time to juggle responsibilities, to create a balanced life that worked. Fresh thoughts strolled through my head.

I need to remember to make time for myself —and daddy.

I should really plan our meals better —and eat more fish.

I need to work at staying in touch with friends —and grandmas.

I really should schedule a haircut...

I shut the door. I unzipped my modern-marvel, electric breast pump and placed it on the desk. I attached the hoses. I assembled the cones. I located an outlet. I plugged in the apparatus and … realized I'd worn a dress. A one-piece long dress, carefully selected for my first day back. It had no waistband to skirmish with my middle, no zipper to fight. I had selected a simple pull-it-over-my-head-and-off-to-work-I-go dress. Hi ho.

Simple.

Until I needed to pump.

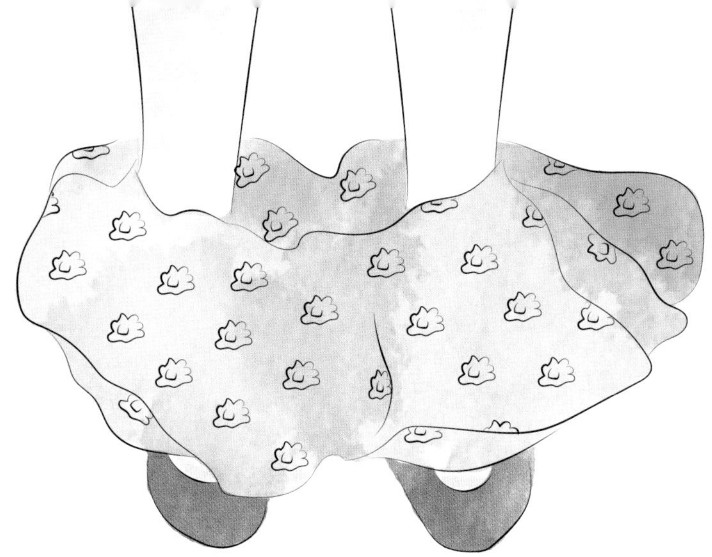

<cue cursing>

You've got to be kidding me.

There was no possible way to access my bulging boobs. I had wasted precious time worrying someone might catch a glimpse of skin peeking from my shirt. Not so. No, if someone opened that door, they would get the X-rated screening. I would be *naked,* with only my far-from-sexy granny panties to shield my post-baby body. (See chapter on exercise.)

I felt like ~~a stripper~~ an idiot as I dropped my dress to my ankles. Grabbing the pump, I settled warily into my office chair, fully understanding this gig would take some getting used to. Maybe I didn't have it all figured out just yet, but I *had* to believe it would get easier. Or, at the least, less, uh, revealing.

Keeping one eye on the door and the other on the ounce marks, I pumped. One miserable drop at. a. time. Exactly twelve ounces later, I turned off the machine and scrambled to pull myself together.

The next challenge? Camouflaging this liquid gold in the office fridge, lest someone mistook it for coffee creamer.

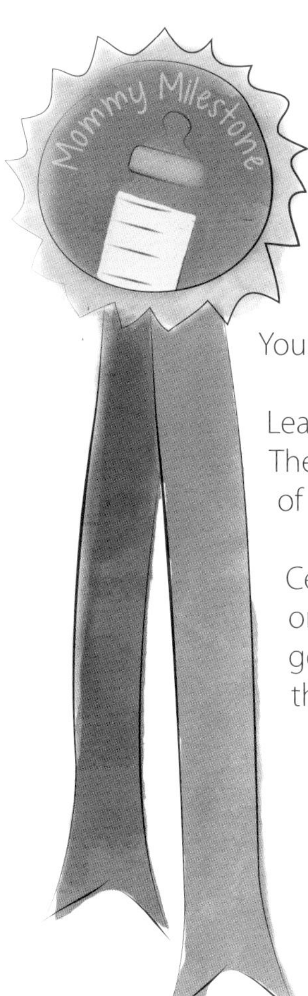

You made it through your first day at work!

Leaving your baby behind is epic. Just remember: There is a precious little someone waiting at the end of your shift. That is an awesome feeling.

Celebrate by kicking off your day shoes, cuddle up on the couch, and grab the remote. Watch a feel-good movie classic and enjoy the simple moments that make life so sweet!

This I believe (most days): We all have awesome skills. You might argue that some are valued higher than others, but when you boil it down, it takes all types of talent to make the world go round.

In the world outside my house, my skills were used for facilitating meetings, negotiating contracts, and networking a room of who's-whos—like a gymnast in a game of Twister. Although considered enviable in the business arena, these abilities were useless in my new role as mom. The Boss wasn't interested in negotiation; he didn't grasp the power of networking; he failed to recognize progress even when it was in front of us for the taking.

Oh, sure. Spit up just as we leave the house.
And all over my shirt. No problem.

But, next time, could we cooperate for once and get our tails out the door?

On time?

<deep breath>

Daycare professionals running his home-away-from-home had a different skill set, one that went beyond my wildest imagination. Simply watching them work the Infant Room as a team was almost magical.

- Managing diaper changes for a party of twelve.
- Facilitating mealtime for nine-month olds (without anyone—young or old—needing a change of outfit).
- Coordinating naptimes so that everyone slept (same time, same place) for two hours. Every day. Without fail.

Their mad skills kept the center under control, and parents like me simply kept out of their way. They distributed reasonable guidelines for us to follow.

1. Baby should be feeling 100%. Keep fevers, sad tummies, and thrush at home.
2. Inform us when baby will arrive late or be leaving early; we will worry and call if he doesn't show up.
3. Bring items from home to keep your baby comfortable. (See our simple Supply List.)

Thank you,
The Wizard Staff

They made it easy for me to follow directions. Frankly, after reading their short supply list, I questioned why we needed so much paraphernalia at home to survive. Was I the only one that needed three changes of clothes, a baby swing, and a bouncy contraption to make it through a day? Obviously, their skills aligned with their goals for a streamlined center. Who was I to probe the whys and hows? My job was to hand over The Boss to these masters.

SUPPLY LIST:
Extra outfit
Favorite blanket
Pacifier (if using)
Two bottles
Fitted crib sheet

Clearly, we served a different clientele. Theirs required sustenance, shelter, and safety; mine sought profits, success, and paid time off. Imagine my excitement when, just as I felt my mothering skills were at an all-time low, I found the talented team in a sticky situation. You can bet your fresh diaper I was happy to step in, roll up my sleeves, and make myself useful in their Maslow's Hierarchy-driven world.

The Facts:

At the end of each week, blankets and sheets were sent home to be laundered. Every Monday kick-started the week germ-free. So it was bound to happen, inevitable really: The door of opportunity opened 52 x per year x 12 little clients at that very spot.

The Situation:

You are doing your laundry—with your favorite fabric softener, dryer sheets, or static guard. Regardless of your secret sauce, physics trumps and clothes cling. When you're dealing with a crib-sized fitted sheet, those corner pockets are magnets. The odds of a foreign object falling into the perfect trap was unavoidable.

The Crime:
One ordinary Monday, all the crib sheets arrived fresh from the weekend. When fluffed for naptime, out flew a pair of undies—a sheer, lacy thong that would make any kid proud. The Wizards were caught off guard with the R-rated scene.

What exactly is it?
What sheet did it escape from?
Who is going to pick it up?
What would the Baby Whisperer do?

While hunting a missing onesie in the center's lost and found, I snagged the lacy thong—and reminded myself that we all have awesome skills: Knowing when a squalling baby needs a toy versus an ear exam is one thing; knowing when to place a thong in the trash rather than the lost and found is quite another.

That afternoon I exercised my own mad skills. After a laugh and a toss, I took care of the misplaced undergarment for the staff.

Next, I decided to buy myself a new thong … to replace the one that had gone missing the week before.

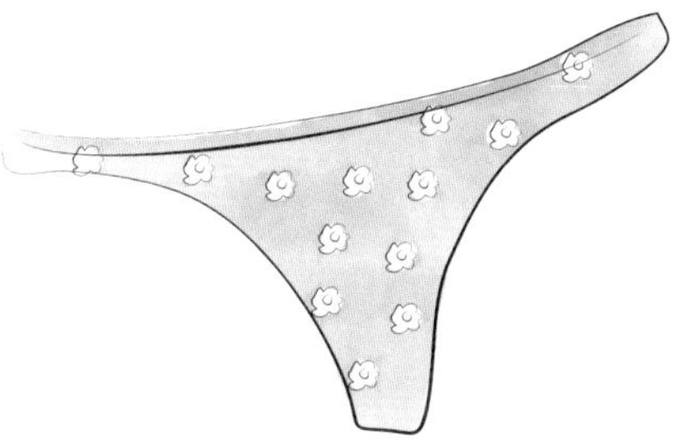

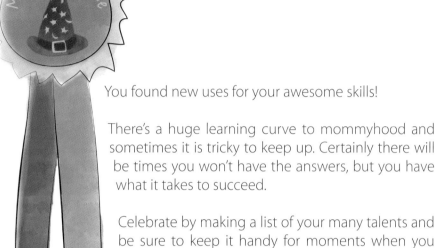

You found new uses for your awesome skills!

There's a huge learning curve to mommyhood and sometimes it is tricky to keep up. Certainly there will be times you won't have the answers, but you have what it takes to succeed.

Celebrate by making a list of your many talents and be sure to keep it handy for moments when you need a reminder. Then, it never hurts to take a quick inventory of your underwear drawer!

I will forever remember the day I realized what utter desperation feels like. I had plenty of past experiences that set the bar fairly high.

Take the time (please, *take* it) The Boss leaked BM during my niece's graduation ceremony and I hadn't packed a spare outfit. Or the morning I stepped on the scale, after eating nothing but leaves for an entire week, and discovered I gained three pounds. And, most memorable, the moment at the grocery store when I realized that the offensive smell I noticed was actually coming from *me*.

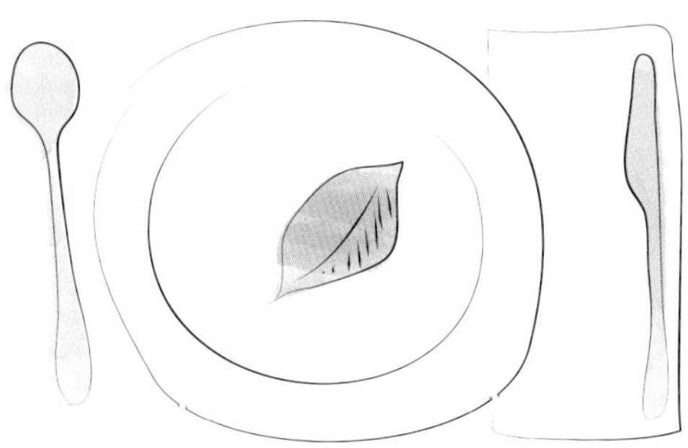

All very desperate situations, you understand, but none was as painful as the hour I discovered my breast pump no longer sucked.

I finally had gotten the hang of pumping at my office, planning my agenda around my daily quota goals, and calculating the exact number of drips necessary to supply the next day's stash. My body was trained to let down, release, and produce. I was amazed. It's just one of the many miracles of the human body I'll never understand. If I could only channel that same power for more good in my world.

Function with four hours of sleep.
Drop those last ~~twenty~~ ten pounds.
Stop growing hair under my ...

It was a Tuesday.

It was time to plug in and rig em' up, as I had done many times. I held the cones to my eager spigots and—witnessed the most pitiful attempt at suction I had ever seen. Fear washed over me. I turned every knob, unplugged and re-plugged, unscrewed and re-screwed anything and everything that could possibly come apart.

Nothing.

In desperation, I called the hubs. You remember him? The fella who bought this amazing invention of mankind? The guy who works with technology every day? He'd know what to do. Right?

Me: My pump isn't sucking. Not sucking. It isn't sucking, I said!

Him: Slow down. What are you talking about?

My breast pump isn't sucking anything and I'm about to explode!

Don't panic. Did you try turning it off and on? Did you check the power supply?

Are you kidding me? Of course I did! What else have you got?

Um, I bought it at the wellness store on Thirty-second Avenue. Maybe that's a place to start?

A place to start? ~~I am a ticking time bomb with no idea will happen if I don't get this FIXED IMMEDIATELY~~!

Thanks for your help.

Buttoning my shirt, I flew out the door and headed, straight arrow, to the birthplace of that blasted machine. I reached the health and wellness shop in record time, only to find a twenty-something *kid* single-handedly running the place during the lunch hour. I threw the bag onto the counter, unzipped it, and pulled out the sad sucker.

Now, this shop sold a wide variety of items, and in a small, hidden corner, they had the pump on display. So I shouldn't have been surprised when the clerk looked at me with a blank stare.

Me: This isn't working.

Kid: What is it?

~~Please don't make me leap over this counter and hurt you.~~

It is a breast pump.

Oh. I think we sell these.

You do. We purchased this here and, no, I don't have the receipt on me. Don't ask.

Did you try turning it off and on? Did you check the power supply?

<silently cursing him> Yep.

Lots of hoses and little flaps that could cause trouble, aren't there?

<Silence>

My manager should be back in an hour. He might have some ideas.

~~Until this is fixed, I will be breathing down your neck and dripping on your counter.~~ Trust me, you don't want to see me in an hour.

I was tempted to demo the contraption but realized that would get us nowhere. He seemed to think that maybe we should start with a phone call to the company and see where that took us. Brilliant.

I followed him (uninvited) to the back office where he called the Pump God. That day, my new best friend and I learned a bit about physics, how those teensy flaps need to be replaced every now and then to create a magical ability to suction fluid out of tiny holes that happened to be growing by the second and begging for some action. Good to know.

Three minutes and $1.47 later, I was on my way out the door, already pretending this never happened.

You can get through desperate times and live to tell about it!

You've found yourself in some wild situations that required quick thinking, common sense, possibly a garbage can, or, at the very least, a magic wand. Those are the episodes you'll giggle about—when the shock wears off.

Take time to laugh at your circumstances. You will later, anyway. So go ahead and find humor in the moment and appreciate the times when "nothing out of the ordinary" seems to sum up the day!

Mommy Milestone

Grasping at Straws and Caffeine

Addictions are everywhere—some good, others not so much.

The Boss loved his pacifier to the point of addiction by some standards. Well-meaning friends ~~lectured~~ informed me about the (lack of) pros and *all* the debilitating cons. But, hey, I was more interested in keeping the screaming Boss … well … *pacified.*

I had my own addiction, vital to my daily existence. Hot, blood-bouncing, energy-infusing coffee. Joe. Java. *My* pacifier of sorts. Going without it for a day was uncomfortable. Struggling moments were soothed by its strength. And, my favorite escape: If I couldn't say anything nice … I'd take a sip.

Coffee simply made me feel better. Smarter. It made me warmer, possibly cuter, definitely more charming. So I was caught off guard when the addiction sneaked in. Not that I cared much. I started out as a social user. Blame peer pressure. I could have taken up golf, I suppose, but coffee was easier to master, less work, and better insurance that Daddy and I would stay together for years to come. I drank coffee all day long and could still fall into a coma-like sleep on command. I was sure I had everything under control; certainly I could stop using at any time and be fine.

Pretty sure.

While pregnant, I listened as the nurse detailed guidelines for growing a baby. No argument from me; this was a big deal. The obvious health tips would benefit everyone:

1. Cut back on late nights.
2. Continue exercising (or maybe start).
3. Hold off on Happy Hour.
4. Take your vitamins.
5. Don't inhale anything inappropriate.
6. Go easy on the caffeine.

Epiphany struck. I opted to go straight—and break up with my pacifier. Cold turkey.

Trust me. Regardless of having my addiction "under control"—it wasn't a pretty sight.

Oh, I will miss you dear coffee,
but experts agree it is for the best.

<exit coffee>

<enter exhaustion>

<enter The Boss>

<enter delusional>

I followed the advice of the professionals and successfully completed a self-inflicted detoxification program. A mere 253 days later, The Boss was delivered without the shakes and I was caffeine free and no longer pregnant. It had been *months* since I had a real coffee. Not the watery decaf I'd used to trick myself. At times, I felt like an imposter trying to hang with the cool kids, but I was proud of the fact that I'd gone straight.

Now what?

Do I go back to the pacifier and live a life of dependency?

Do I continue on my path of freedom, charging on to bigger and better (if there is such a thing)?

I found myself struggling. It was like that terrible stage of growing out your bangs until they are almost—but not quite—long enough to tuck behind your ears and you need to make a decision. How badly do you want them? Are you going to have bangs the rest of your life? Or are you going to persevere and make a difference in that Christmas card photo for once?

I had come so far. I could accomplish anything I put my mind to. Or maybe anything I put my mind to might be a stretch.

I have a disorganized house with stacks of laundry thrown about.

I've got no meal planning skills.

I will never admit to the size of pants I am wearing.

Clearly not basing my decision on past successes, I decided to go for it. I chose the high road. I would start drinking water for a change. I might make a nice cup of decaf tea every now and then or grab a lemon to really class it up. That's right, no room for pacifiers in *my* life. I was moving on. Go big or go home.

Sure. I might catch a sip every now and then. But don't wait around, Cool Kids. This mommy was growing out her bangs, er, kicking the habit. And no one was going to stand in her way!

<still delusional>

About a ~~week~~ minute later, I did the math and realized I hadn't had a full night's sleep since The Boss moved in. I thought of the constant limitations and pressures I faced: foods to steer clear of (gassy side effects) and adult beverages (no more happy hour).

Thanks for the reminder, lactation consultant!

And let's not forget that I was now working full time, not only required to arrive at the butt-crack-of-dawn but also expected to stay awake the entire day. I missed the guilty pleasures of my glory days.

It was a moment of decision and I made it. I owned it.

I sprinted to the coffee pot. I poured a mug of fully leaded. You know, the stuff dreams are made of, straight from the jungles of Columbia or the mountains of Folgers. Whatever.

Ahhhhhh.

I held the hot, delicious mug like I had just won an Olympic medal. I could almost hear chanting friends pounding the table, cheering me on.

The reunion with my addiction was historic. Probably because I was able to stay awake for it. Not only did coffee get me through that day, but through an evening with The Boss and, best of all, through the final stages of growing out my bangs.

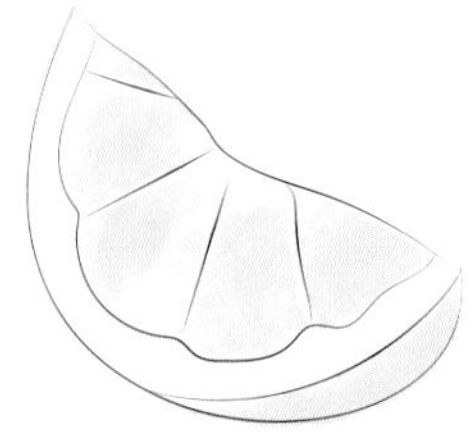

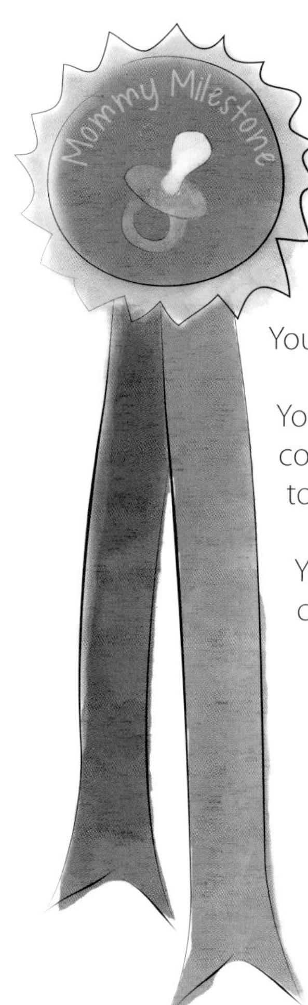

You get to decide what's in your life!

You might find times when you feel you've lost all control. Don't let anyone fool you, you have the ability to make choices without excuses.

You know what's vital to your world; be proud of your choices and celebrate with your favorite indulgence!

I needed to make a quick trip to the grocery store. But past experience had proved nothing was quick with The Boss as co-pilot. I preferred to solo. In record time, I went through the checkout line and found myself with a rare fifteen spare minutes looking me straight in the eye and flirting. I had a choice to make.

Option #1: Pick up The Boss early from daycare.
It would be a nice change of pace from my usual arrival out of breath, screeching into the Friendly Frogs Room seconds before the hourly rate became a by-the-minute-knock-your-socks-off premium.

Option #2: Make one more stop.

Conveniently located next door to the market was a wine and spirit shop. The idea of grabbing a bottle (or two) and arriving home with something other than the familiar and predictable 2% standard beverage was appealing.

I'm going to be really honest. My life doesn't typically involve leisurely wine drinking. The thought of having wine on hand for a ~~fingers-crossed~~ just-in-case moment was almost as good as a planned date night.

It's time to switch it up a bit. Daddy will be so surprised:
picking up something out of the ordinary;
showing I took some initiative;
proving I still have some imagination;
hinting I have a little something up my sleeve.

It's time to pay attention, Big Guy.
I'm practically making a move.

If a simple bottle of wine could inject a little excitement, I was game. Besides, it was time to remember we owned glasses made of, get this, *glass*. And that was almost as exciting as what we'd pour into them.

I stole those fifteen precious minutes to wander the aisles of wine country. Instantly, I was on holiday, reading exotic labels that whisked me to far-a-way places. I pretended to know what I was hunting. Maybe a wine ~~imaginary~~ dinner guests would appreciate? A wine that might look best on our table or, heck, as long as I'm pretending, a wine that would fill a hole in our collection? A helpful clerk interrupted my fantasy.

Helpful Wine Expert: Is there anything I can help you find today?

Me: No, I'm doing fine. Thanks anyway.

Well, maybe I can help you find a nice wine that would pair well with tonight's dinner?

Dinner? That's a nice thought.

What are you planning for dinner tonight?

<enter my blank stare>

Don't panic, I chastised myself. Just think of something normal to say. What normal people eat for dinner. Chicken. Beef. Fish. Pasta. Just pick one already. It was a normal question. I looked like a normal person who eats a normal dinner.

Gosh, it was almost like a compliment.

He actually thought I was going to go home and have a nice dinner with my family, sit around the table enjoying a well-prepared, nutritious meal, share exciting details of our day.

Maybe, somewhere, that was how dinner worked. Yeah, like in Never-Never Land.

Me: Corndogs. We're having corndogs.

Helpful Wine Expert: Really? Well, that's a new one. Let me know if you need any help.

Idiot. Corndogs. Really?

Just like that, my daydream was over. My secret was out. Any worldliness I portrayed was snatched from my grasping, greedy fingers.

Remembering The Boss, I blindly grabbed the two nearest bottles of wine, forked over a credit card, and raced out the door.

Sorry, daycare teachers.
You won't be going home early tonight.

That evening, we dined on corndogs. And they were awesome. I pulled out stemmed goblets and poured wine for a toast. I suddenly understood that *every* day was worthy of using the nice glasses, no matter what we drank from them.

Even with something on a stick. Dipped in ketchup.

You realize every day is special!

Managing the basic needs of your family, you find it's easy to get trapped in a rut. The moment you realize how a little gesture can put a fun twist to a typical day is pretty exciting. You don't need to wait for anniversaries or promotions to do something special and out of the ordinary.

Pull out your glassware (or go buy some) and fill them with your beverage of choice. Make a toast to celebrate the best-day-ever moment found in the everyday with those special people who sit around your table.

Breastfeeding a newborn was a bonding experience like no other; I got on board with that. What I could get even more on board with? Last call. The light at the end of the nursing tunnel. Reclaiming ownership of my boobs and my social calendar.

Now, I realize I was the one person in charge of everything nursing related—including the timeline—and, don't get me wrong, I loved bonding, the hands-down convenience, and the feeling that I was doing something only I could for The Boss. At the same time, I really missed having any scrap of control over my

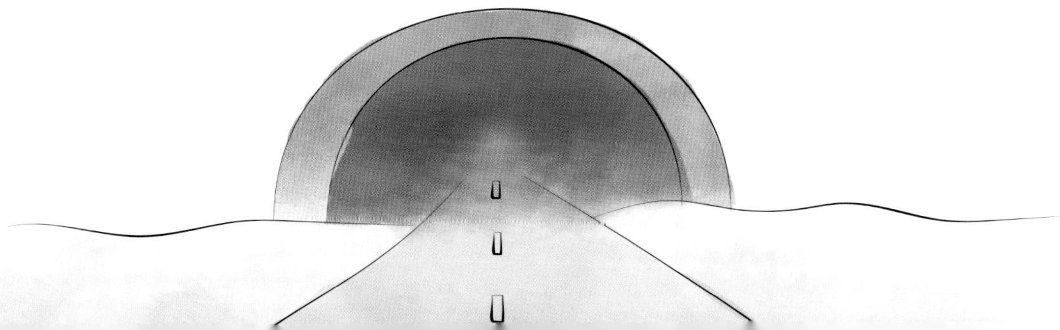

schedule and was starting to obsess over the increasing quantity needed to meet the demands when we were apart.

The early days of our nursing adventure seemed so long ago. I had come a long way, with priceless memories ~~burned into my mind~~ etched forever on my heart.

Late night feedings and sleeping in the rocking chair.
Cuddling after he spit up everything he just guzzled.
Camouflaging my liquid gold in the office fridge.

Him: Why are you crying?

Me: I pumped all this milk and spilled it over the counter and now I don't have enough for tomorrow and there isn't any way I can ever get these six ounces back. EV-ver!

Okay, okay, calm down. Just use some that you put in the freezer.

But that is our reserve stash. For emergencies and when I am not around.

Umm, isn't that what this is?

<tears>

And remember, "Don't cry over spilt milk."

And there was the time the in-laws came for dinner. When one small request for Grandpa to lend a hand and grab extra ice for our drinks led to the discovery of the century. Curiosity exploded around the mound of small, frozen bags in our freezer. Curiosity—and probing questions about my stash. Move over, Barbara Walters.

What is all this?
How do you get extra milk?
How long does it take to build such an impressive inventory?

When he invited Grandma to admire what daughter-in-law had produced, I felt like a prized Holstein. Although I will agree it was an impressive sight. Needless to say, our dinner conversation was just as ~~inappropriate~~ lively. Grandpa suddenly recalled working on the dairy farm as a kid growing up. Add that to my glory days in the local 4-H Club, and there is no doubt this milk supply feat was blue-ribbon worthy at any county fair.

While fully supportive of my decision to stop nursing, my husband was quick to inform me just how much three ounces would bring on eBay if I wanted to extend the duration for extra cash.

Regardless of the potential for an exotic vacation destination ($$$$$), my shift was over. It was time to park the dairy truck.

Last call, kiddo, 'cuz I'm tapped out.

I was ready to move on to my next bonding adventure, fingers crossed that this time I could keep my shirt on and it wasn't going to hurt.

You are ready for the next stage!

Congratulations on realizing you have the option (when you and baby are ready) to progress to another adventurous level. Whether it's feeding methods, sleep routines or something between, you're moving on.

Capture this graduation moment with a photo op of you and the babe. Time to focus on the future!

I keep a clean enough house, but nothing compared to my mom's. (No, hers is an entirely different level of clean. Award-worthy, actually). Housework isn't my passion. Rather, it's a necessity I can appreciate—then put off to the last possible moment. Which would be when ~~my mom~~ company comes for a visit.

I was wicked good at a quick game of pick-up and could fool any who arrived on short notice. On the surface, the house appeared comfortable, cozy, and organized. I graciously took jackets, seated my guests in view-limited chairs, served beverages, and kept the conversation ball rolling. Rolling far, far away from my messy reality.

<behind the scenes>

Quickly shut cupboards, closets, and doors leading to other rooms.

Never let anyone open the dishwasher.

Ditto with the pantry, the oven, the refrigerator, the washing machine.

Oh, I knew guests weren't completely oblivious, but at least they kept mum about their thoughts and opinions. Honestly, true friends were easy to woo because they already knew details around my cleaning schedule.

Me: How often does a person need to clean her oven?

True Friend: That depends on when you moved in. How long have you lived here?

My mom, however, was a visitor of a different mold. Her superpowers pinpointed the exact spots I didn't want her to notice. The minute she stepped foot inside our door, I rushed to justify how busy the past few weeks had been and how quickly the house duties had gotten away from me. She pretended indifference. I could tell she was rarely impressed.

But the moment she stepped in wearing her New Grandma badge, things changed. Her superpowers sharpened to higher levels, and it was clear that the Little Boss was deserving of the best and she was going to remind me. Every. Single. Day.

I cleaned.

I bought products. I procured tools. I managed to scrape the reserves of my flailing energy. I did what I could to meet the strict guidelines set by grandmas around the world to protect these precious beings. I may have breezed over some areas from time to time but, cards on the table, you would have found yourself in an honest-to-goodness, germ-free, pine-scented, kick-your-pants-all-the-way-to-the-bathroom, sparkling house.

That's right, Grandma. Check that off your list. *One time ever.*

Then things got worse.

No need to panic. Not a thing I can do about this.
It was in all the books. Bound to happen.
The Boss is on the move, and there's no stopping him now.

Chalk up one more life-changing event.

In a blink of an eye, the world was now The Boss's playground and, it seemed, his dinner plate. Floors once merely a stomping ground for our grubby street shoes became his turf, staked out for creeping, crawling, rolling, kicking, slapping, pounding, licking and, yes, sucking. Nothing was off limits. He didn't discriminate. Anything and everything he could get his pudgy hands on went in his mouth, a novel game of Finders, Eaters.

The day I found him exploring a huge potted plant, I dialed an old friend.

Me: I have a quick, hypothetical question for you
Ask-a-Nurse: Yes, what is your question today?
Let's say a baby ingested some dirt. Could that possibly be a problem? Just curious.
This isn't an emergency?

Oh, don't be silly. But, if some baby were to get some dirt accidently in his—or her—mouth, what advice would you give?

Hypothetically.

No need for alarm. He was going to be fine and actually looked the happiest I had seen him in a long time. I stopped worrying and started cleaning mud off The Boss, then mud off the couch before Daddy got home to ask questions.

The Boss' explorations stretched my own, and I learned to embrace his development. A growing, moving baby meant ~~chaos~~ change and, lucky me, I got to race after him—and ahead of him—as our boundaries widened.

And remember all that cleaning? Even that definition altered as I figured out what I could safely camouflage and what needed to be removed from my baby's reach. (Thanks, Ask-A-Nurse.)

Some moms are fiends for freshness and passionate for polish—and I love visiting them! But in my world, freshness arrived via aerosol spray and the only thing polished was the floor—courtesy of a little fella's knees.

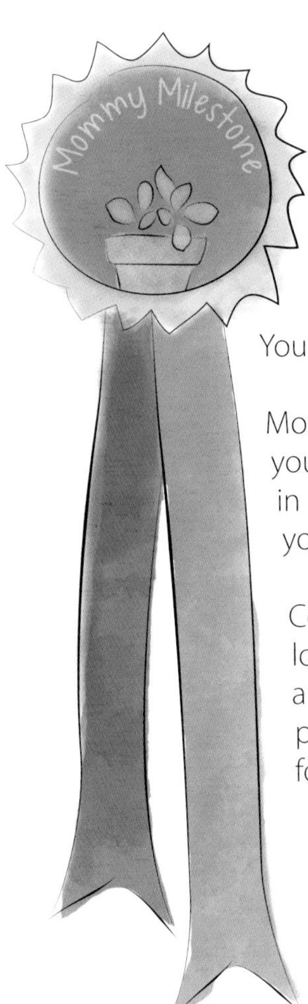

You are wise to what matters!

Mommyhood can make your head spin. You prioritize your days by acknowledging that with every change in your baby, you are becoming wiser, quicker on your feet, and ready for his—or her—next step.

Celebrate by treating yourself to a service that allows you a little extra time. Home grocery delivery, a detailed car wash, lawn care, or a few hours of professional housecleaning will give you a break to focus on and enjoy something that matters to you!

A lot of hard, crazy, horrendous things happen over the course of a year, as well as a lot of growing, changing, and learning. It's all amazing, really. Wildly amazing.

The Boss is turning one!

There is much to celebrate:

He started walking.
And, if my eyes wavered from him for even a second, he tumbled right into the center of the earth.

He slept through the night.

Which may or may not have been an accurate statement. No matter, he was safely confined to his crib so I was mostly okay with him crying it out.

He ate on his own.

He grabbed table food by the handfuls and most of it made it to his mouth. The rest smeared his face, clothes, every crevice in the highchair, and the floor.

He loves to smile.

At me. At Daddy. At random strangers. Even at plants.

I started to build a blueprint for this once-in-a-life time celebration:

1. Invitation list: The Boss didn't have many friends, so I took the liberty of inviting all my BFFs.
2. Menu: A taco bar felt festive, tossing in some kid-friendly finger food (plenty of that around my house).
3. Music: Reggae was a hit. Bonus? The Boss bounced to the beat and would never notice that the ABC song didn't make the party mix.

4. Drinks: Margaritas obviously paired well with a taco bar. And cheers to Crystal Light for making a great five-calorie version.
5. Theme: Okay, The Boss had this one. He liked balloons and could say "ball" so we played off that.

Reviewing the list, I wondered if I was making this party a little too much about me.

Seriously, he won't even know what day it is.
He got his way with the theme.
I promise to snap a ton of pictures of him smearing cake.
That should do. Right?

I stopped worrying. The past twelve months were filled with crazy and exhausting things I had done to keep us functioning. While carefully charting Baby Milestones—careful not to miss a precious event, I couldn't help but think about the powerful Mommy Milestones that I had reached and survived. In the span of one year, I found myself drastically changed into a better person now planning a party for my one-year-old.

I was ready to celebrate my Mommaversary, the One Year Anniversary of *my* life-changing event.

The day you remember exactly where you were
when you started to feel a little "uncomfortable."

The day you scrambled to grab your perfectly packed bag
and checked into the hospital.

The day your water broke, nurses became your angels,
and labor happened as ~~planned~~ nature intended.

My priorities shifted. It wasn't all about me anymore.

I became a stronger person inside and out:
Infant carrier + diaper bag = workout.

I realized the importance of others in my life,
treasured friends and family.

I learned to really appreciate the small things in life like sleep,
a hot meal, stretchy pants.

I discovered a broader admiration for my husband,
and I dug to a deeper understanding of myself.

Amazing. I made it. I made it through an entire year. And I have a huge photo album to prove it!

You laughed along the way. You cried along the way. Now, it's time to take the opportunity to recognize all of the awesome Mommy Milestones that have taken place throughout the year—those everyday-moments that make life so special.

It is time to host your One Year Mommaversary party filled with friends, food, and fun to celebrate your achievements, your growth, and your awesome self!

Cheers to You!

Mommy Milestones is growing and we'd love for you to join us as we ~~stumble~~ find our way through of all the awesomeness that happens in this ever changing world.

If you are looking for ways to connect with a community of those who like to celebrate the crazy everyday good in life, find us at: www.mommymilestones.com. Here, you can share YOUR milestones (both old and new) and register your Mommaversary to receive treasures throughout your journey of motherhood.

Here at Mommy Milestones, we know not everyone is planning a dream family vacation … we believe there are ways you can have Your Best Day Ever within your already amazing life.

The good stuff is all around us … sometimes all you need to do is plug your nose and dig a little deeper.

To connect with the creator of Mommy Milestones: